THE QUEER DUTCHMAN

TRUE ACCOUNT OF A SAILOR
CASTAWAY ON A DESERT ISLAND
FOR "UNNATURAL ACTS" AND
LEFT TO GOD'S MERCY. . . . .

GREEN EAGLE PRESS
New York

The Queer Dutchman Castaway On Ascension

by Peter Agnos

THE QUEER DUTCHMAN, CASTAWAY

Printed in the United States of America

1993   (C) 1978 C. Adler

ISBN 0-914018-03-5

GREEN EAGLE PRESS
BOX 20329, CATHEDRAL
NEW YORK, NY 10025

TEL: 212-663-2167
FAX: 212-316-2261

qd-isbn.625

Preface to the Reader

Four winters ago, while browsing in Mendoza's Bookstore on Anne Street in lower Manhattan, I chanced upon a curious old book written in Dutch. The illustrations of old sailing ships, of shipwrecks and of men and cargo floundering in the sea caught my eye, and I bought the book. My friend Michael Jelstra, who was born and raised in Delft, told me that the old volume was a copy of sea adventures published in Amsterdam in 1762. One story in particular intrigued me that of Jan Svilt, who was forcibly marooned on Ascension Island in 1725. Michael translated the original journal into English for me. I have added various explanatory notes and comments which I trust will add to the reader's understanding and appreciation of the journal.

Nullius in verba
Peter Agnos,
Sonora, Mexico
May 1977

CONTENTS

This book is based upon a journal kept by Jan Svilt who in 1725 was forcibly marooned on the deserted island of Ascension. Svilt's journal was found by Captain Mawson, Commander of the British ship Compton, homeward bound from India. Mawson had stopped at Ascension to turn turtles.

How strange a crazy-quilt of fate is the life of man and by what hidden currents are the affections hurried about as conditions change...

Robinson Crusoe

VERSCHEIDENHEID MAAKT VERDRAAGZAAMHEID

The 130ft. Dutch East Indiaman *Geertruyd*.

I. The Trial of Jan Svilt

The following report was taken from the records of the Dutch East India Company, Algemeen Ryksarchief VOC.* (It was translated by M. Jelstra from the Captain's report.)

Second of May 1725. To the Most High Seventeen.**
Report of Captain Dirk van Kloop, master of the *Geertruyd.*

At seven hours after Midday, after the evening prayers, *Oppersturman* (first mate) Pieter Graff entered my cabin and in a most distraught manner asked me to speak with him. Our conversation went as follows:

"Sir, it has been reported to me that two of our crew have been engaging in the sins of Sodom and Gomorrah." This charge filled me with much apprehension. I asked: "*Oppersturman,* how did you come to hear of this?"

*Vereenigde Oost-Indische Compagnie
**The directors of the Dutch East India Company

"Two seamen who witnessed the abomination told me of it," he said. "They are Johan Eckoff of Delft and Nicholas Fockema of Leiden. They wait outside to testify and to swear to what they have seen."

The two witnesses were asked to enter my cabin. I called a council of the *Geertruyd's* officers to hear the evidence. Ordinary seaman Johan Eckoff has been with the Company for six years; ordinary seaman Nicholas Fockema has sailed with the VOC for nine years. This is the story to which they swear.

"We had attended the evening prayers on deck, conducted by Spiegel the Ziekentrooster (catechist), at which he read to us a portion of Paul's Epistle to the Romans. After the psalm, which he sang off-key, and because it was a very hot evening with no breeze, we two walked about on deck awhile and then repaired to the head. After that we two went 'tween decks to find our pipes. It was already dark in the crew's quarters. As we approached our hammocks in the forecastle of the ship, only one small candle cast a dim light.

"We noticed that the furthest porthole was slightly ajar. As our eyes became accustomed to the dark, we spied two bodies close to the porthole through which streamed some moonlight. As we moved silently towards the bow, we made out two men with their shirts off sitting close to each other. They seemed to be looking out at the moon. The bigger man, who was Jan Svilt, had his arm about the waist of the smaller man, Bandino Frans. We saw them turn their heads towards each other, put their mouths together and engage in a long and passionate kiss.

"When we observed their monstrous behavior, Nicholas Fockema started to hoot and giggle, whereupon the two men sitting on the deck stopped their hugging and sinning and turned towards us.

"We jeered at Svilt and Bandino. We called them buggers and queers and said that they must squat to piss. The boy said nothing, but Svilt called us syphilitic boors, pimp-bait, drunken louts, and other unkind names. We then decided to report what we had seen to *Oppersturman* Graff.''

As Captain I was greatly distressed by the remarks of seamen Eckoff and Fockema. The abominable sins of homosexuality can, as attested in the Bible, bring ruination to our community, as they brought down the wrath of God on Sodom and Gomorrah. I requested the petty officer to bring Svilt and Frans to my cabin to stand trial. A council of ship's officers was convened to hear evidence.

When all the officers had been gathered for the trial, the two witnesses repeated their story under oath. The accused men denied that they were doing anything improper. The boy, who was my mess boy, and is young and innocent, appeared flustered, blushed and said little. Svilt, when his turn came to testify, denied that he was doing anything against the laws of God or man. He did not deny that he had had his arm around Bandino's waist or that he had kissed him. He defended himself thus: "Bandino has been like an adopted son to me since he came aboard in Batavia. I have protected him from the drunken bullies, of whom Eckoff and Fockema are the worst on this ship. I have kept Bandino from the syphilitic Company's Slave Lodge in Capetown. I have watched over him as a father.

"Life on this ship is hard, and Bandino is not used to the ways of Dutch seamen. I promised his uncle that I would look after the boy until he reached Holland. My affection towards him has been as a father to his son, and in no way improper.''

The ship's council doubted that Svilt was telling the whole truth and decided to apply an appropriate torture to delve for the true facts. Since neither Bandino nor Svilt were willing to confess, the council decided to place burning fuses between the fingers of the accused. But they remained adamant and would no more confess.

The council then decided to subject Svilt to the water-cure: Svilt was tied to a mast and a canvas sheet was secured around his neck. Water was poured into the sheet until it covered his mouth and nose. Svilt swallowed considerable amounts of water for the first hour of the torture. His belly distended enormously, but he kept declaiming that he was a God-fearing man and that he was innocent. At the urging of the officers, however, more water was poured around his head until he fainted. When he revived, he confessed.

"I am drowned. I will tell you anything you want. What do you want to hear? I will tell you anything your filthy ears would like to hear."

These insulting remarks towards the ship's officers did not go down well with the council. Svilt then confessed to having had abominable sexual relations with Bandino—the recitation of his confession caused us to shrink from him in horror. These deeds are of a dangerous and abominable nature that ought to be punished by death so as to prevent future evil. Some of the officers felt that if homosexuality on the ship was not quickly rooted out, terrible plagues might strike our ship, discord would grow among the seamen and God would take from us all that is good.

We might have punished both wrongdoers by tying them together and tossing them into the sea—a just and proper reward for Sodomites. But because of the youthfulness of Bandino Frans and because of the closeness of our fleet to Ascension Island, the full council of the ship, with the agreement of the Commodore of the fleet, resolved with the greatest speed to place Jan Svilt upon the desolate Island of Ascension and let God punish him as He would. Accordingly, when the fleet hove into sight of Ascension, Jan Svilt,along with his gear and food and a cask of water was placed in a long boat and rowed to a southwesterly Bay, where he was set on shore.

Signed: Capt. Dirk van Kloop, followed by 20 signatures.

THE FLAG OF THE DUTCH EAST INDIA COMPANY.

D T Valentine's Manual 1863

16

II. The Diary That Jan Svilt Kept on Ascension Begins

By order of the Commodore and Captains of the Dutch fleet bound home from Callicut, I was set ashore this 5th of May upon the Island of Ascension, which struck me with great dread and dissatisfaction, but I trust that Almighty God will protect me. They put me on shore on a sandy beach which faces towards the west with a cask of water, a hatchet, two buckets, a banjan*, a quilt, some peas and rice and,few other necessities.

* * *

I pitched my tent on the beach** near a conical rock on which I set my duffelbag of clothes as a marker so that I might better know where to find them. The weather is clear and dry. Towards dusk I climbed a hill covered with rocks and cinders. I could see still the sails of the Dutch fleet as

---

*A loose-fitting Indian shirt.
**Svilt was put ashore at Clarence Bay.

they moved slowly north towards Holland. For the first time since I left Amsterdam two years ago, I am completely alone...God preserve me.

On Sunday, the 6th, I climbed to the tops of barren hills to see whether I could discover any living creatures that were good for food, or any greens whereby I could satisfy my raging hunger; but to my great confusion and sorrow I found nothing. There seems to be little life on this island. As I gazed on the desolate landscape I sincerely wished that some accident would befall me, to finish my miserable days with little suffering.

In the evening I walked back to my tent, but at first could not find my way. Melancholy, I walked along the strand praying to God Almighty to put a period to my days—or help me off this desolate island. I found my tent and secured it against the weather the best I could with stones and a tarpaulin. About four or five o'clock, I killed three birds called boobies. I found salt on rocks above the spray line. I skinned and salted the birds and put them in the sun to dry. These sea birds, with their grey feathers and sad brown eyes, were the first things I killed upon this island. The same evening I caught two more birds, which I served as before.

My captain assured me that ships from the Indies sometimes stop at Ascension to turn turtles or repair leaks.

I have set my flag, made from an old red shirt, upon the highest hill overlooking the water. I will keep a strict calendar and journal so that I may know the sabbath and the holy days.

Why did I return to the sea? When I was twenty and sailed on the *White Elephant* to Batavia, the sea filled me with wonder. I was drawn to her like a child to its mother, and she gave me a chance to see the wide world before I settled down with my wife.

Then the sea let me feel my strength, sail with other strong young men, run up and down the shrouds and whistle at the ocean winds. But now I am thirty-nine years old. God has punished me for returning to the sea. How have I sinned?

III. Ascension as Seen Through the Eyes of Other Early Seamen and Adventurers

Few sailing ships stopped at Ascension during the early days of sail. They preferred to lay over at St. Helena, 800 miles to the south—a well-watered, pleasant and populated island. Early accounts of mariners who visited Ascension help explain why it was usually avoided.

From HAKULYT POSTHUMOUS we have the following two accounts:

In 1600 John Davis wrote:

"This Isle has neither wood, water nor greene thing upon it, but is a fruitlesse greene Rocke of five leagues broad..."

Sir James Lancaster stopped there in 1603 and wrote in his journal:

"No ships touch at this Iland for it is altogether barraine, and without water: only it has a good store of Fish about it, but deepe water and ill-riding for ships."

In 1696 Robert Everard, on a voyage from India, noted:

"...in our way we touched on an island called Ascension which shows itself like a burnt cinder. Here we stopt to take in some turtles as most English ships do that come this way."

William Dampier, the sometime pirate, naturalist, and writer, was shipwrecked on Ascension in February, 1701. His ship, the *Roebuck,* sprang a leak, and with the help of an inept carpenter, sank. Here follows his account:

"I asked the Carpenter's Mate what he thought of it; He said 'Fear not; for by 10 a clock at Night I'll engage to stop the Leak.' I went from him with a heavy Heart; but putting a good Countenence on the Matter, encouraged my Men, who pumped and bailed very briskly; and when I saw Occasion, I gave them some Drams to comfort them. About 11 a clock at Night, the Boatswain came to me, and told me, that the Leak still encreased; and that the Plank was so rotten it broke away like Dirt; and that now it was impossible to save the Ship."

Dampier and his crew toiled all night. The next day they sailed in close to shore, then carried a small anchor ashore and warped the ship in until she was in only three and a half fathoms. Dampier continued:

"...I made a Raft to carry the Men's Chests and bedding ashore; and before 8 at Night, most of them, were ashore. I had sent ashore a Puncheon, and a 36 Gallon Cask of Water, with one Bag of Rice for our common use: But great Part of it was stolen away, before I came ashore; and many of my Books and Papers lost.

"On the 26th following, we, to our great Comfort, found a Spring of Fresh Water, about 8 miles from our Tents, beyond a very high Mountain, which we must pass over: So that now we were, by God's Providence, in a Condition of subsisting some Time, having plenty of very good Turtle by our Tents, and Water for the fetching."

The site of Dampier's spring is probably Breakneck Valley, the main source of the island's present limited water supply. This runs southeast, and is often beset by fog clouds round the peak of Green Mountain. To reach it one must climb a 2400-foot ridge.

Dampier and his men survived, living on turtles, land crabs, sea birds and goats. During their explorations they found a "shrubby tree" chained to an anchor, with the date '1642' carved on it.

On the 3rd of April, three British men-of-war, together with the *Canterbury,* an East Indiaman, anchored in the bay. Dampier and thirty-five of his men sailed for England on the 9th of April, 1701. They were lucky.

In his account of his adventures, Dampier noted:

"Ascension is without wood, water, or herbage but some hogs and fowle and abundance of turtles and fish...a blot on the fair surface of the earth, an awful wilderness in the solitude of the ocean."

Ascension is a dismal spot. A Portuguese traveler with d'Alberquerque who saw the island in 1503 said of it: "The place was of no use as far as we could tell, and we left it behind us." The Dutchman Jan van Linschoten came by but did not land on the island in 1589. He commented on the birds: "...so many birds...the bigness of young Geese came by the thousands flying about our ships crying and making great noise and running up and down in the shippe, some leaping and sitting on our shoulders and arms... We took many of them and wrung their necks but they are not good to eat because they taste fishy."

Almost all visitors land on the western side, which is sheltered from the prevailing easterlies. The beaches there are fine white sand. In 1673, when the English overran St. Helena and captured 300 Dutchmen, they at first planned to leave the captives on Ascension, until a Dutch ship came by to take them off. But the English relented when they found no water on the island.

IV. Svilt Explores Ascension

On the 7th in the morning I went to my water cask, which was full half a league from my tent, and broached it, by which I lost a great quantity of water; but afterwards turning the cask upon its head, with much difficulty I saved the rest. I employed myself for the remaining part of the evening in carrying stones to make my tent the stronger.

On the 8th early in the morning I took down my flag in order to place it on a hill the other side of the island. In my way thither I found a turtle, which I killed with the butt end of my piece, and returned back to my tent to rest my limbs, still flattering myself that some ship or other would speedily come to my deliverance. At night I removed my tent to the other side of the rock, being apprehensive of the destruction threatened by the moldering stones that were impending and unwilling to be accessory to my own death, trusting that God would still permit me to see better days. There was not a more commodious place on the whole island where I could have pitched my tent, which was no small satisfaction to one who labored under such deplorable circumstances. And what illustrated more the beauty of divine Providence, I still enjoyed my health. In the evening I killed more birds.

On the 9th in the morning I went to search for the turtle I had killed the day before, carrying my ax with me and split it down the back, it being so large that I could not turn it whole: cut some of the flesh from off the forefin which I carried to my tent, salted and dried in the sun; and having a second time screened my tent with a tarpaulin, I began to build my bulwark of stones about it.

On the 10th in the morning I took four or five onions and a few pease and carried them to the south part of the island to find a proper place for them, looking carefully all the way on the sand in order to discover a rivulet of water or the footsteps of some beast, by whose track I might in time find out the place where they drank. I also diligently sought after some herbage, and after a tedious walk over barren sands, hills and rock, almost inaccessible, I discovered a little purslane, part of which I eat for my refreshment. And being both weary and thirsty and having no water to drink, put the remainder into a sack which I had with me. In returning to my tent I found some other greens, but not knowing what they were did not dare to eat of them.

On the 11th in the morning I went into the country again and found some roots which had a taste not unlike that of potatoes, but was apprehensive they were not wholesome. I endeavored to make other necessary discoveries but to no purpose, which made me very disconsolate. Being almost choked with thirst, I returned to my tent, which was situated on the side of a hill, near which was another hill of a larger size, and adjacent to that a sandy bay. Upon the largest hill in the evening I boiled some rice, being much disordered in mind and body.

On the 12th in the morning I boiled some rice again and, having eat a small quantity, offered my prayers to God for a speedy deliverance. I then went towards the shore in hopes of seeing some friendly vessel approaching but found none; then walking on the beach till I was weary, seeing nothing but empty shells, returned to my tent. It was my usual custom to walk out every day in hopes of a distant view of ships upon the ocean, forced by stress of weather to make towards this desolate island to repair their damages. Afterwards I read Lamentations till I was tired and employed the remainder of the day in mending my clothes and the chief part of the night in meditations and dismal reflections on my unhappy state.

God's grace has cast me away on a barren island midway between Guinea's coast on the east, and Brazil to the west. The closest bit of land is St. Helena, 800 miles due south. My tracks around the island thus far have filled me with dread: I fear the whole island may be barren and rocky, destitute of useful vegetation. I did spy a greenish mountain towards the center of the island and will explore it. Many extinct volcanoes dot the bleak landscape. I have seen little but grey and brown rocks and a dry grey soil which might produce crops if there were sufficient water.

Along the northeast strand near to the great grey cliffs, I spied a great colony of rats, animals that I abhor.... Great long waves roll against the grey cliffs, exploding with great force and making a booming noise as if God is calling to me.

How different is this barren place from the Holland where I was born and lived most of my life. There it is always damp. In the winter the canals freeze over and I would ice skate for hours with hundreds of other bundled-up Amsterdamers. And then we would go to the inns and drink big pewter mugs of beer....

The rats I saw today reminded me of an awful event from my childhood. When I was twelve, my father, who made his living then as a rat catcher, apprenticed me to a bookkeeper in Amsterdam. But before that he had left me with the family of Jacob Vlekke, a miller of Delft, while my father, who had been a brave soldier in the wars against the French,* travelled around the country catching rats. Holland was then suffering much from a plague of rats, who ate the grain in the millhouses, the seed in the ground, the flour in the bakeries and any other food they could gnaw into.

I was in Vlekke's barn. My father had asked me to guard an enormous wire basket of rats hanging by a chain from a large beam overhead. Excited little bodies scurried about; beady rat eyes peered at me, snake-like tails pointed at me. The large vanes of the mill cut off the light intermittently, as the rats swished past the mill window. I went over to the cage and looked closely at the 2 dozen fat

*The Nine Years' War pitted the Dutch, with their sometime ally England, against France. The French were brilliantly effective on land, and their great pirate, Jean Bart, and his Corsairs destroyed many Dutch merchantmen. But in 1692 the British and Dutch fleets soundly defeated the French navy under Count Tourville in the harbor of La Hogue, now called The Hague.

THE HARBOR AND CITY OF AMSTERDAM.

rats. The cage swung over my head; suddenly the chain broke— The cage with its wild rats hit me in the face as it fell, knocking me down. The cage door sprang open and the hoard of rats clambered over my body as they escaped, helter skelter, to the fields. Just then my dear father came in. He picked up a cudgel and beat me till I was black and blue and could hardly walk... The rats on Ascension are bold and move in large packs. I covered my food with large rocks to keep it from them.

V. Ascension: Svilt Plants a Few Seeds and Decides to Collect Specimens for a Natural History Cabinet

On the 13th in the afternoon I put the onions, together with some pease and calivances, into the ground near my tent, to try if they would grow.

The 13th early in the morning went in search of some sea fowls but found none. In my return back along the beach I found a turtle, with whose eggs and flesh I made an excellent dinner, boiling them with some rice. I buried the remainder that could not be immediately used, for fear the stench should offend me, the turtle was of so large a size that it is impossible for me to eat it whole whilst sweet. I also found some buried nests of turtle eggs, which I boiled, melting some of the fat of the turtle to mingle with them, burning the remainder of it in the night in a saucepan, not having a lamp.

On the 14th after prayers I took my walk as usual, over the grey rocks, but finding nothing new returned to my tent, mended my clothes and continued writing this my journal.

On the 15th, before I took my walk, I ate some rice and then followed my usual employment, viz. the catching of those tame sea birds called boobies. I afterwards amused myself with reading a book of travels and then endeavored to ease my tortured mind by a calm repose.

On the 16th and 17th I caught several of the small grey terns, one of which I kept alive for the space of eight days. But it wanted its freedom and it died.

On the 18th two more.

The 19th nothing worthy of note.

The 20th caught one booby bird.

Today I decided to collect specimens of rocks and animals and plants from this island and to prepare a *raritenkamer* (cabinet of curiosities). It will help occupy my lonely hours and with God's help, should it please Him to save my miserable life, I may be able to sell my specimens to a wealthy merchant in Holland. Many an Amsterdam burgher considers himself a patron of the arts or sciences and will pay good guilders for unusual collections.

When last I was in Amsterdam I read George Rumphius's *Amboinese Raritenkamer,* published some twenty years before. This most beautiful and fashionable volume detailed the minerals, shells, birds and beasts of Amboina, where the blind seer had been stationed for many years. The book sold many copies at a high price. If God could grant a blind man the sight to collect and illustrate hundreds of natural samples and to write that great work, perhaps He would grant me the strength— and the time—to catalog, the miserly life on this, His and my desert island prison.

Enormous flocks of sea birds live in the rocks and cliffs near the shore. They appear to be mainly of two kinds, terns and boobies, but occasionally I have spied men-of-war and other large birds. I can discern that they have no natural enemies here—if one excludes the rats who eat their eggs and their young in the nests. The birds are not afraid of humans and allow me to walk among them so it has been easy to capture them. I have collected samples of their feathers and eggs.

I also have collected samples of rocks: grey, black and brown, which are exposed throughout the breadth of the island, but I do not know their names.

Towards the eastern side of the island there rises steeply a greenish tinged peak. The upper slopes of this mountain support a meager vegetation. Little greenery shows elsewhere. As yet I have collected but three kinds of grass and plants* and three small land crabs.

All is cindery, desolate and flat on the western part of the island. I have counted over 40 extinct volcanic cones protruding through the bleak landscape. Rocks are most always ash-grey, black, brown or rust color. I see nought but desolation, chaos, petrified mounds and jagged rocks, which have cut through my leather boots. Overhead the tropical sun blazes on a desert of sterile lava, heating it hot enough at midday to cook kugelcake. What I would not give for a slice of kugelcake and a mug of beer!

---

*James Cunningham made the first botanical survey of Ascension in the 1690's. He could find only four kinds of plants. The scarcity of native flora is due to the relative geological newness of the island and its great distance from other areas. The dryness of the climate does not encourage growth. According to Cunningham, the only native animals are land crabs, turtles and seabirds.

VI. Ascension: A Fire and Other Hardships. The Roaring Torrent of the Ocean.

The 22nd, after breakfast I went to the other side of the island to try to make some discovery, but came back as I went— with nothing. In the afternoon took my line and fished from a rock near four hours but had no success. At my return, my tent, to my surprise, was filled with smoke. I remembered that my tinder-box was left upon the quilt. The smoke smothered me so greatly I could not enter the tent. I hastened to the sea-side for a bucket of salt water and soon quenched the flames. I return God thanks that all my wearing apparel was not burnt, having lost nothing but a banyan shirt, the corner of my quilt and my Bible singed; I entreat God Almighty to give me the patience of Job to bear with my present afflictions.

The 23rd: this morning I remade what was burnt

yesterday then I marched bravely over the black sands
singing at the top of my lungs:

> *I will praise my Lord, thy grace,*
> *Fountain of all power;*
> *Thou art in storm my sheltering place,*
> *My salvation tower.*
> *What if men assail me?*
> *What if men assail me?*
> *God, my Lord will break their sword;*
> *He will never fail me.*

Only the boobies and the terns listened; they did not
seem impressed. If God heard me, He did not indicate yet
that He approved of my conduct.

I learned that hymn when I was a child in Delft; it was
my favorite hymn. Now the sun is setting far away over
Catholic Brazil, and I do not feel like singing bravely. Lord
have mercy.

The rest of the evening I spent in admiring the infinite
goodness of Almighty God, who had so miraculously
preserved the small remainder of my worldly treasure; and
sometime tortured myself with the melancholy reflection of
the punishment God has reserved for me. I well know the
wages of sin are death, but I could not possibly form an
idea in my mind of a punishment that could justly atone
for my offence.

The 24th I walked to my flag and returned again to my
tent, having caught one booby only, which I broiled on the
embers and eat.

On the 25th after breakfast I went to catch sea fowls, then returned to my tent and dried them.

The 26th I repeated my usual endeavors in order to descry some ships sailing on the ocean, but to my great disappointment found my hopes frustrated; neither could I find any fowls or eggs that day. On the 27th met with the same ill success.

The 28th I went the west side of the island and I ascended a hill so high that had my foot slipped I had inevitably been lost, but found nothing remarkable nor any food wherewith to satisfy my craving appetite.

On the 29th and 30th I met the same disappointment.

On the 31st I secured the provisions I had before salted and laid in the sun to dry and was forced to feed on them.

From the 1st to the 4th of June it would be needless to relate how often I strained my eyes, misled with distant objects, which the earnest desire of my delivery made me believe to be some ships approaching. Every little atom in the sky I took for a sail. The roaring torrent of the ocean*, intermixed with the sun's bright rays, presented to my view a yellow gloom, not much unlike the moon when part obscured. The streaks of the element and every cloud seemed to me as a propitious sail. But reflect how dreadful was the shock when from my tired eyes the object flew and left behind sad scenes of black despair.... When I was put on shore the captain told me it was the time for ships to

---

*Rollers, huge breaking-waves, smash with great noise and violence into the volcanic northern cliffs of the island. The great waves are formed by storms in the North Atlantic which cause a swell to move outward from the storm's eye. Longer waves travel faster and maintain their energy longer than shorter, choppier waves. The regular long swell waves can move thousands of miles outward from a storm and carry with them enormous energy in their rise and fall. The waves strike the gray cliffs of Ascension like thunder claps.

pass that way, which made me more diligent in my search.

From the 5th to the 7th I never failed to take my usual walks, along the shore to look for ships—although in vain. Near noon I went to a conic mountain a good way off the place where I landed. It was steep and of difficult access, because with each step the sand and stones rolled down. The heat increased, and I was forced to rest several times... Neither on the sides, nor at the top, did I meet with one single plant; on the summit, where the air was very cool, stood a pole three fathoms long, which was provided with the necessary ropes for hoisting a flag. From the pole hung a wooden cross, which had the letters I.N.R.I. carved on it.

VII. Capetown: Outward Bound

How did it happen that Svilt, a God-fearing bookkeeper with a wife and two daughters in Holland, should find himself on Ascension in such desperate straits? To answer that question it is necessary that we examine Svilt's journal to see what he was up to before he landed on Ascension. This chapter and those about Batavia should clarify the situation.

First of June, 1724. Lookout in the crow's nest sighted the sugar-loaf mountain of Capetown. When he called down to the crew "Capetown, Capetown", they swarmed to the rail like flies to a pot of honey and cheered the sight of land. We had been at sea for four months, our water is low; our food stale and rotten. Many good men had died of the scurvy and others were too sick to work. The sick and dying below decks cheered as best they could, for Capetown was the only hope of many that they would survive. Twenty-five men had died since we left Holland. Three had fallen from the yards, two had died of wounds in Snikersnee, the remainder had succumbed to diseases of one kind or another. Thirty-two men lie ill below decks. I thank the Lord that I am still sound.

We anchored in Table Bay amidst 20 other vessels moored in the roadstead; ships from England, Denmark, and the Arab lands flew their bright flags in the African sunshine.

Most of the men shaved and trimmed their scraggly beards; some of the crew even bathed, though most consider it unhealthy to wash away the essential body oils. We perfumed ourselves and put on our best clothes in preparation for our descent onto the "Tavern of the Seven Seas." Midway between Holland and the Indies, the Cape, to us, is a refuge with fresh food, women, and good hospitals—a refuge without which we probably could not survive.

Capetown was first settled around the year 1650 by the Company to provision and assist Company ships. But many Dutch settlers have started farms and keep vineyards and cattle and trade with the natives against Company objections. Despite the protests of the Herren XVII,* the Cape recently was made a Dutch colony.

The promontory of the Cape consists of a high, flat-topped plateau which affords a welcome view to the sailor at sea. Without doubt it was this agreeable prospect that prompted the Portuguese, who first found the route to the Indies, to stop here. For many years their sailors coasted south along the vast continent of Affrick towards the South Pole until they sighted the Cape and could then veer to the east. They named the promontory the Cap de Bon Esperance or Cape of Good Hope. But the Portuguese never settled here, preferring to victual on an island nearby.

*The seventeen high directors of the Dutch East India Company.

38

Now industrious husbandmen grow plentious supplies of wheat, barley, pease, and fruits of many kinds: apples, quinces, pears and the largest pomegranates that I ever did see. The chief fruits are grapes, which thrive well, and the country of late years is so well stokt with vineyards that they have overabundance of wine and do sell great quantities to passing ships.

With my crewmates I came ashore and invaded first the Red Ox and then the Blue Anchor which lie near the quey. These taverns are all run by former Company servants who have taken to drink themselves, as indeed, alas, have too many of our settlers. Three sailors and I entered the Last Penny Tavern half tipsy and before the evening was up, we had spent most of our pay on wine and gin. We caroused and sang, then staggered into the streets, where we met sailors from all corners of the earth. Full of good cheer, four of us wandered over to the Company's whore house, and though the dark girls were indeed comely, I had little desire for them for fear I would catch the French pox. Lucas and I did stand outside weaving from side to side, holding each other up looking at the pretty mulatto girls. I thought of my wife and two girls in Holland; I wished I was with them there...

The second day ashore I visited my companion Jil at the hospital, which hereabouts is called the "Cemetery." To my relief, Jil had visibly improved since he was carried from the ship. The fresh food and land air had caused his scurvy skin sores to partially heal and though he had lost four good teeth to the disease, his gums now were firmer and he could eat solid food. He said he would wait for another ship to the Indies and that I should call on his mother should I arrive in Holland before him, which was likely.

After wishing Jil godspeed, I joined some of the crew who were at the wharf unloading goods from Holland:

cookware, cloth, bricks and two cows. Since I am the ship's bookkeeper, one of my jobs is to keep account of the cargo that enters and leaves the hull. Aboard the ship there is much contraband that I cannot mention. The *Oppersturman* told me that he saw two high officers enter the house of a rich burgher with sacks over their shoulders. He saw them leave an hour later with smiles on their faces.

We remained at the Cape for twenty-two days, taking on cargo, fresh food and water. With one hundred sixty-three men we sailed eastward into the Indian Ocean towards Batavia and the Indies.

Ships in Table Bay — Capetown

VIII. Ascension. Water Grows Scarce. Svilt Finds a Small Stream.

On the 8th my water grew so scanty that I had but two quarts left, and so thick that I was obliged to strain it through my handkerchief. I then, too late, began to dig in the middle of the island, and after digging six or seven foot deep could find no moisture. I then returned to my tent and endeavored to make a new well, but found it impracticable. After having gone a fathom deep my grief was inexpressible to find no water to relieve me from this desolate island, where there is nothing left that can long sustain a human creature.

On the 9th, found no manner of food. I passed away my time meditating on my future state.

On the 10th I boiled some rice in the little water I had remaining, having little hopes of any relief but perishing. I recommended my soul to the Supreme Governor of all things. But recollecting that I had formerly heard there was a well of water on this island, whilst I was able to walk I traveled over hills and rocks to the other side of the island, being determined to leave no place unsearched.

Despite the hardships aboard my ship, I wish I were on her now. Of the 200 men that sailed with me from Texel two years ago, 30 died of scurvy before our first landing at the Cape. Forty more men died of miasma in that stink hole, Batavia. Aboard the *Geertruyd* the rats are ferocious, and the bedbugs sucked my blood every night. I complained to the cook of the the monotonous diet of beans and onions, with meat only twice a week, oversalted cod and bad water. But now I see that it was a paradise compared to this blight of an island.

Today I went to the crest of one of the high peaks of the many extinct volcanoes, got on my knees and prayed. Some small grasses grow here, but no trees. To the south is another peak with a green tinge on its slopes. The remainder of the island is like a burnt cinder. I believe that the island is shaped roughly like an equal-sided triangle, with the small base facing west and its point facing Africa. I would judge that the base is six miles long; the sides of the triangle somewhat greater.

This evening, after saying my prayers, I looked to the west. All at once the entire sky was darkened by a great cloud of sea birds rising in unison. Thousands upon thousands of terns and boobies rose from the rocks where they breed and flew together as if guided by some unknown master. The only enemy of this innocent flock are the rats, no doubt introduced here by the Portuguese, when they first landed here on the day our Lord ascended to heaven.*

The winds blow steadily again from the east, dry and

---

*Svilt here refers to the fact that the island was first discovered by the Portuguese mariner Juan de Nova Costella on Ascension Day, 1501.

hot, as they invariably have. The cruel sun beats down, heating the barren stones underneath. My wife and friends in Amsterdam would envy me this warm sun and mild climate; it is probably raining in Holland. Friends? I have no more friends except perhaps Death. He waits on the other side of the green mountain. Why do I not now go to join him? Let me meet Death head on, for there is no hope. Dear Savior, if I look him in the eye, he may fly from me.

After prayer and four tedious hours' search, my tongue was parched; the intolerable heat of the sun made my life a burden to me. But I proceeded though very faint, and almost dead with heat and excessive fatigue. Then God in His gracious goodness led me to a hollow place in a rock, from whence issued forth a stream of fresh water.

It is impossible for me to express my great joy and satisfaction at so agreeable a sight. I drank to that excess as to almost hurt myself, then sat down by the current for some time and drank again. After which refreshment I returned to my tent, having no vessel to carry any water away with me.

On the 11th in the morning, after returning my sincere and humble thanks to the Maker of all things, I took my teakettle, together with some rice and wood, to the place where the spring was, and there boiled my rice and eat it.

On the 12th I boiled some rice for my breakfast and afterwards with much trouble carried two buckets of water to my tent. My shoes being worn out, the rocks cut my feet in a terrible manner, insomuch that I was often in danger of falling and breaking my buckets, without which I could not possibly live.

On the 13th I went out to look for food but found none, but chanced to meet with some little weeds like birch, which I brought to my tent and boiled some rice for my dinner. After which I walked to the seashore to look out as usual, but my flattered hopes created in me a deep melancholy.

IX. On the Marooning of Sailors During the Age of Sail, with Particular Reference to Alexander Selkirk

The marooning of mariners because of natural disasters was fairly common when sailing ships plied the oceans. DeFoe's *Robinson Crusoe* chronicled a not unusual experience of his times when it was published in 1706. Jonathan Swift's hero, Lemuel Gulliver, encountered four different disasters which put him ashore on remote and unexplored sections of the globe. *Gulliver's Travels* appeared in 1726, one year after Svilt was cast away on Ascension. However, Svilt's case was somewhat unusual in that he was forcibly put ashore by his officers, who condemned his sexual proclivities.

The most famous 18th century British castaway was Alexander Selkirk, a thirty-year-old Scot who was put ashore on Juan Fernandez Island in 1708 at his own request. After Selkirk had had irreconcilable differences with his captain, he chose to trust to his own fate on a small island off the coast of Chile rather than sail with such an impossible commander in a poorly kept ship.

Juan Fernandez was a well-watered island with lush trees, cats, and goats that fortunately could be caught. According to the journal of Woodes Rogers*:

---

*Woodes Rogers: A Cruising Voyage Round the World, 1712.

"...He diverted and provided for himself as well as he could; but for the first eight months had much ado to bear up against melancholy and the terror of being left alone in such a desolate place. He built two huts with pimiento trees, covered them with long grass and lined them with the skins of goats, which he killed with his gun as he wanted so long as his powder lasted, which was but a pound; and that being near spent he got fire by rubbing two sticks of pimiento wood together upon his knee. In the lesser hut, at some distance from the other, he dressed his victuals and in the larger he slept and employed himself in reading, singing psalms and praying; so that he said he was a better Christian while in this solitude than ever he was before, or than, he was afraid, he should ever be again. At first he never ate anything till hunger constrained him, partly for grief and partly for want of bread and salt; nor did he go to bed till he could watch no longer. The pimiento wood, which burnt very clear, served him both for firing and candle, and refreshed him with its fragrant smell.

"He might have had fish enough but could not eat 'em for want of salt because they occasioned a looseness; except crayfish, which are there as large as our lobsters and very good. These he broiled, as did his goat's flesh of which he made very good broth...

"He came at last to relish his meat well enough without salt or bread and in season had plenty of good turnips which had been sowed there by Captain Dampier's men and have now overspread some acres of ground. He had enough of good cabbage from the cabbage trees and seasoned his meat with the fruit of the pimiento...and also a black pepper called *Malagita* which was very good to expel wind and against griping of the guts.

"He was first much pestered with cats and rats that had bred in great numbers from some of each species which has got ashore from ships that put in there to wood and water. The rats gnawed his feet and clothes while asleep, which obliged him to cherish the cats with his goat's flesh; by which many of them became so tame they would lie about him in hundreds and soon delivered him from the rats. He likewise tamed some kids and to divert himself would now and then sing and dance with them and his cats; so that by the care of Providence and vigor of his youth, being now about thirty years old he came at last to conquer all the inconveniences of his solitude and to be very easy...

"The climate is so good that the trees and grass are verdant all the year. The winter lasts no longer than June and July and is not then severe... The heat of the summer is equally moderate... He saw no venomous or savage creatures...

"By this one may see that solitude and retirement from the world is not such an insufferable state of life as most men imagine, especially when people are fairly thrown into it unavoidably, as this man was, who in all probability must otherwise have perished in the seas, the ship which left him being cast away not long after and few of the company escaped...

"A plain and temperate way of living conduces to the health of the body and the vigor of the mind, both which are apt to be destroyed by excess and plenty, especially of strong liquor and the variety as well as the nature of our meat and drink; for this man when he came to our ordinary method of diet and life, though he was sober enough, lost much of his strength and agility. But I must quit these reflections, which are more proper for a philosopher and divine, than a mariner..."

Richard Steele, who knew Selkirk in England after his return from Juan Fernandez, wrote of him:

"This plain man's story is a memorable example that he is happiest who confines his wants to natural necessities... to use Selkirk's own expression, 'I am now worth eight hundred pounds, but shall never be so happy as when I was not worth a fathering!'"

Not everyone in Europe felt that Selkirk had been happy in

his solitude. The sometimes-mad English poet Cowper used Selkirk's experience to build a poem of great strength which is more in keeping with the solitude of Svilt than Selkirk.

I am monarch of all I survey,
  My right there is none to dispute;
From the centre all round to the sea
  I am lord of the fowl and the brute.
O solitude! where are the charms
  That sages have seen in thy face?
Better dwell in the midst of alarms
  Than reign in this horrible place.

I am out of humanity's reach.
    I must finish my journey alone,
Never hear the sweet music of speech,
    I start at the sound of my own.
The beasts that roam over the plain
    My form with indifference see;
They are so unacquainted with man,
    Their tameness is shocking to me.

Society, friendship, and love
    Divinely bestow'd upon man,
O had I the wings of a dove
    How soon would I taste you again!
My sorrows I then might assuage
    In the ways of religion and truth,
Might learn from the wisdom of age,
    And be cheer'd by the sallies of youth.

Ye winds that have made me your sport,
    Convey to this desolate shore
Some cordial endearing report
    Of a land I shall visit no more:
My friends, do they now and then send
    A wish or a thought after me?
O tell me I yet have a friend,
    Though a friend I am never to see.

How fleet is a glance of the mind!
    Compared with the speed of its flight,
The tempest itself lags behind,
    And the swift-wingéd arrows of light.
When I think of my own native land
    In a moment I seem to be there;
But, alas! recollection at hand
    Soon hurries me back to despair.

But the seafowl is gone to her nest,
    The beast is laid down in his lair;
Even here is a season of rest,
    And I to my cabin repair.
There is mercy in every place,
    And mercy, encouraging thought!
Gives even affliction a grace
    And reconciles man to his lot.

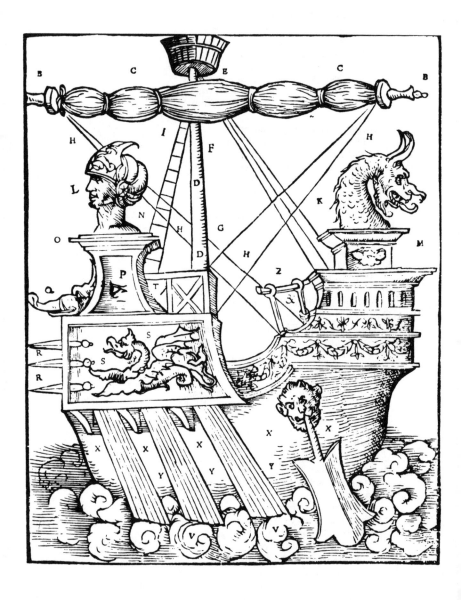

X. Svilt's First Nightmare. Life Aboard the Geertruyd.

On June the 14th I took my teakettle and some rice to the watering place where the water was. After having refreshed myself I returned to my tent, mended my clothes and spent the remainder of the day in reading the Bible.

15th. All the day employed getting of sea-fowls, eggs, and birds.

On the 16th I took my walk on the beach as usual and with as little success as ever, then returned to my tent to repose myself, where in the solemn gloom and dead of night I was surprised by uncommon noises surrounding my tent. Bitter cursing and swearing mixed with the most blasphemous and libidinous expressions that I ever heard. My hair stood on end with horror and cold sweat trickled down my cheeks. Trembling I lay, fearful to speak, least some vile fiend more wicked than the rest should make a prey of me. I fear that the Devil has forsook his dark abode and come attended by infernal spirits to keep his hell on Ascension, for I was very certain there was not a human creature on the island except myself, having never observed the footsteps of a man since my being there.

Their discourse and their actions was such that nothing but devils could be guilty of; one more busy than the rest kept such a continual whisking of his tail about my face that I expected nothing less than to be instantly torn to pieces by them. Among the rest I imagined to have heard the voice of a friend of mine, with whom in this lifetime I was very conversant. Sometimes I imagined myself to be agitated by an evil spirit, which made me cry to the Almighty for succor and forgiveness of my sins. I believe it was near three o'clock in the morning before this hellish tumult ceased; and then, being weary and spent, I fell asleep. About seven I arose and returned thanks to God for my safe deliverance, but still heard bitter shrieks near my tent. Yet could I see nothing. Then, taking my prayer-book, I read those prayers proper for a person in my condition; at the same time heard a voice saying, "Queer, Asshole fucker, Asshole fucker!" I cannot afford paper enough to set down every particular of this unhappy day.

I would not be in this miserable state if Captain van Kloop had not subjected me to the water cure.* After hours of drowning and gasping for breath in his hellish contraption, I would have confessed to buggering not only his darling cabin boys, but the whole Dutch navy. I am innocent before the Lord; though my affection for Bandino perhaps went beyond that of an older friend.

---

*The "water cure" was a form of torture borrowed by the Dutch from the Chinese. The prisoner, who was to confess his guilt, was not beaten or mutilated; he merely had a sort of inverted cape tied about his neck, so that his head was inside the base of a funnel into which water was poured till it covered his mouth and nose. In order not to drown, the victim had to swallow water to lower the water level so that he could gasp air. Then the torturers poured in more water. Difficult prisoners often swallowed enormous quantities of water, which distended their bellies and bladders to the bursting point. Few guilty (or innocent) tongues failed to loosen when given the "cure."

When a man is at sea for two years, away from the love of his family, is it not natural that he should wish to give and take affection to his companions, especially when they are friendly and shaped like a young maiden, as is the beautiful Bandino. And did I not promise his uncle that I would care for him?

The 17th. I fetched home two buckets of water and dreaded night's coming on. I interceded with God Almighty that I might not be troubled again with these evil spirits. I trust God Almighty heard my prayers, for I was not perplexed with them that night.

Before I came upon this miserable island I was a true Calvinist and used to laugh at the Romans when they talked to me of apparitions; but to my great sorrow now find smarting reasons to the contrary, and shall henceforth embrace their opinions. This day, as I stood under the bright sun near the peak of a volcano, an apparition of a man in the likeness of Piek Houtman appeared on a black plateau near me. He conversed with me. I did not know whether to run or to cower, but remained rooted to the spot as he talked to me of the sins of my past life (of which I have a sincere and heartfelt repentance). Houtman's nearness shocked me so that I became unsure whether or not I was already dead, or whether the vision was sent me to prepare me for death. Perhaps the sun has befuddled my brain. I dropped to my knees and prayed to the Father, the Son and the Holy Ghost.

On the 18th, after my devotions, I went to look out as usual and took my hatchet with me; but, finding myself disappointed, made all possible haste to the other part of the island, where to my great satisfaction I found a tree, which I believe Providence had thrown on shore in some measure to alleviate my present misery. I divided it with my hatchet, the whole being more than I was capable of carrying at once. I took part of it on my shoulder, and having carried it halfway to my tent, laid it down and rested myself thereon. Alas! how wretched is that man whose bestial pleasures have rendered him odious to the rest of his fellow-creatures and turned him loose on a barren island, Nebuchadnezzar-like,* to herd and graze with beasts, till, loathsome to himself and spurned by man, he prays to end his wretched days! His guilty conscience checks him, his crimes flare him full in the face, and his misspent life calls aloud for vengeance from on high. Such was the case of me, unhappy wretch, which proves the justice of All-gracious Heaven; and whilst I was resting my wearied limbs and seriously reflecting with myself the apparition again appeared to me, which gave me horror inexpressible.

His name I am unwilling to again mention, not knowing what the consequence may be. He haunted me so long that he began to be familiar with me. After I had rested some time I carried my burden to the tent and returned to fetch the other part. On the 19th I went in the morning to see my colors, where for some time I fed my longing eyes with the ocean in hopes to see some ship approaching, but being denied so agreeable a prospect, when night came on I laid me down to rest and found no interruption by those evil voices which had before disturbed me, nor heard anything of them the next day, which made me hope the damned had reassumed their dismal caves. But when night came on, to my great surprise the restless apparitions grew more enraged and doubled their fury, tumbling me up and down so in my tent that in the morning my flesh appeared like an Egyptian mummy. Piek Houtman spoke several times to

---

*Daniel 5:33. The once mighty king Nebuchadnezzar went to live out his last years and died among the cattle content with his lot.

me, nor could I think he meant any harm, for when he was living we were as friendly as brothers. He was a soldier in Batavia. The saucepan was thrown down, the light put out and all my things left in a strange disorder. I then began to hope that if Heaven did not think fit to end my torments these punishments would serve as an atonement for my desire to make use of man to satisfy my lust, despising woman, which His hand had made a far more worthy object. My death begins to draw near, my strength decays and life is become a great burden to me.

I dreamt I was again aboard the *Geertruyd* scudding before the wind. I had left my books below and had climbed the ratlines to the crow's nest above the main topsail. Above me waved the flag of Zeeland; before and below me I spied the blue and orange ensign of Holland posted above the spritsail topmast. With me in the crow's nest was a young seaman who scanned the horizon for signs of land.

I am saddened by the thought of the men who had died, and who would die to enrich the Company. Many in its employ would die so that the spices and the gold would continue to flow to Holland. Many poor natives would be sold into slavery and many more would waste away their lives so that silks would grace the fine women of the Heeren XVII.

The *Geertruyd's* hold is filled with cloves and nutmeg, mace, cinnamon, ginger and myrrh, which should gladden the hearts of the Company shareholders. Also 200 sacks of sweet sugar, 80 bolts of fine silk and copper from Japan; sapphires and rubies from Ceylon, carved ivories and cotton goods from Callicut. In return for this wealth that will enrich the burghers of Amsterdam, we carried outbound in our holds barrels of slated pork, beef,

herrings and barrels of other salted fish caught in
Freisland, great wheels of Edam cheese; iron bars, trinkets
for the savages; brass cannons, muskets, powder and shot
to maintain our dominion; and, my mouth waters when I
think of it, 200 barrels of wine, beer and strong liquor.
Since I was the bookkeeper on the ship, I know what she
carried. I know also that Captain van Kloop engaged in
private trade, which is strictly against the Company's rules.
In Deshima he traded illegal gold coins for seven ivory
idols.

I dreamt that I looked down from the crow's nest and
saw a gang of sailors attempt to set a spritsail, the wicked
sail under the bowsprit. But a fog came up and clouded
them over. Peter Pine, the Englishman, lost his life on the
outbound journey trying to set the dread sail in a gale as we
left the cape. We never found his body. And young Piet of
Leyden fell from the yards and splashed his skull on the
deck. He was buried at sea. And three *Hooploopers*
(apprentice seamen) died of the scurvy before we reached
St. Helena and were tossed into the sea. But God has
preserved me, a mere bookkeeper. Therefore I trust in His
mercy...

In my dream I gazed over the horizon to the East and
saw the lush African continent with rain falling in torrents
on to green forests. Black Indians swam in the flowing
stream, bathing and splashing water on each other. I took
off my clothes and jumped in the cooling waters; and as I
swam I opened my mouth and drank in the cooling waters.
When my belly was full I sported with the black natives in
the water.

But such dreams could lead to evil thoughts. My
thoughts turned quickly to our sturdy round-bottomed
Geertruyd, 130 feet long and built like a pregnant cow.
Rows of cannon bristle from the main deck and hide

behind shuttered ports 'tween decks. Our hammocks were slung between the cannons. Sand and rocks in the bilges ballast the ship, and hold her steady when the seas wave... The VOC provides severe punishment for men who piss or shit in the hold. Nevertheless many men act like animals and have indeed filled the bilges with foul pestilence and odors. There is always a stench coming from the ship's bowels. Nonetheless, I maintain that the *Geertruyd* is much cleaner than English and Spanish ships I have boarded... Directly on the sand ballast lie the ship's water and wine casks; would that I was with them now... Her rich cargo is stored in the decks above, a cargo that would enable me and the whole crew to live well for the rest of our lives... But my mind is wandering. I again saw the black Indians swimming in the African stream just before I awoke with a great dryness in my throat...

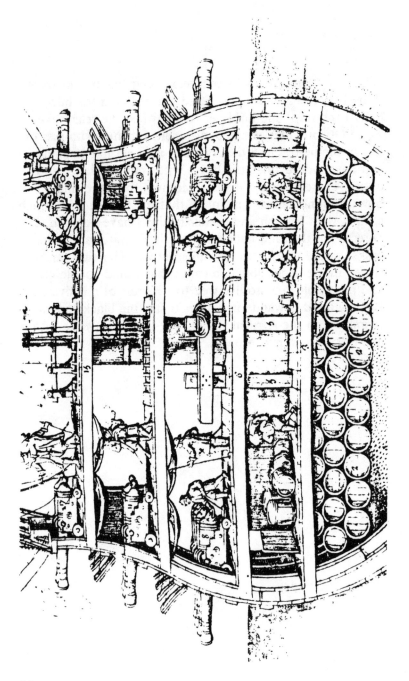

A Cross-Section of Jan Svilt's Floating Home for Two Years

The mizzen-mast, its giant pulley-blocks and its mooring bitts stepped deep in the hull. The ship has four main decks, three 'tween-decks, an upper deck and a hold where casks of fresh water and other provisions were stored on top of sand or gravel ballast. The ship's stores, stowed below the water-line, are protected from enemy fire if the ship is not heeled over. Access passages run the length of the hull. The crew slept on the battery decks. Cannon, decreasing in weight from the lower to the upper decks, are shown level. They would not normally be visible through the ports on both sides of the ship. The crew's hammocks were slung above the guns, usually much lower than shown here. It was difficult to move about beneath them without bumping into the occupants. Note the huge pulley-blocks, one for swaying up the foremast yard and the other for hoisting the mainsail, as well as the heavy bitts for mooring cables about the mast foot.

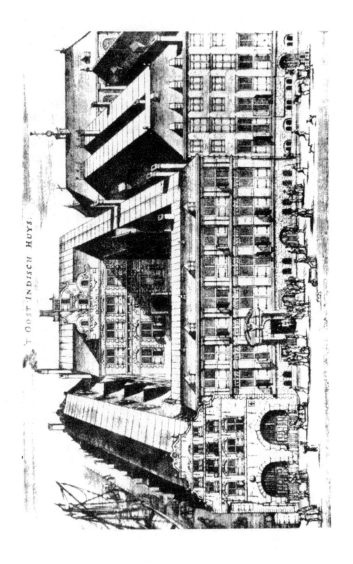

'T OOST-INDISCH HUYS.

60

XI. Holland and Svilt's World

During the 17th century the independent Dutch Republic emerged as the world's greatest maritime and trading nation. The power of little Holland rose remarkably after the devastation of Central Europe during the Thirty Years' War (1618-1648). The seven northern Protestant provinces of the Netherlands, of which Holland was the largest, welcomed the persecuted and the talented refugees from the Catholic world then dominated by the Spanish and the Portuguese. Industrious Huguenots, Jews, dissenters, victims of the Inquisition, even Catholics who expressed unpopular ideas, came to Holland and helped make her the intellectual and industrial hub of the world.

The Spanish Netherlands had long been a center of manufacturing and commerce in Northern Europe, and Dutch merchants were respected throughout the world. Dutch fishermen dominated the North Sea fishery. When, for unknown reasons, the herring moved out of the Baltic and into the North Sea, in 1473 boats from Zeeland and Holland fished the Dogger Bank and Amsterdam was "built on the bones of herring," as weil as oysters, cod and whales. The Dutch sent 7000 ships to the Spitzbergen Islands in the Arctic and harpooned over 30,000 whales from 1675 to 1721.

The struggle of the Dutch for independence from Spain drew men and energy from commercial affairs. Hollanders, who lived in a small, semi-submerged swampy triangle of flatland hardly fit for human habitation, were forced to fight for their freedom against imperial Spain, which for a time ruled half of the Western world. Though the Dutch suffered some of the bloodiest cruelties ever meted out by one so-called Christian sect against another, a combination of thrift, hard work, and an openness to new ideas (coupled with the pigheadedness of the Spanish under the Duke of Alba and Philip II) paved the way for the economic ascendancy of Holland.

Philip's ultimate blunder was to ignore the prosecution of the Dutch war for an assault against England with his "invincible Armada." Many of the Spanish galleons were destroyed by the smaller, more maneuverable Dutch vessels. The Armada's defeat left England and Holland in control of the seas. During the 80-year war against the Spanish, Dutch buccaneers plundered many rich Spanish galleons. In 1648, the Peace of Westphalia recognized the independence of the Netherlands, including the predominantly Catholic Flanders.

As the war slackened in the late 16th century, the Dutch in the northern seven provinces turned with renewed vigor to European and overseas trade. Dutch trading fleets sailed to the East Indies and to the Indian Ocean in the 1590's and overwhelmed the rotting Portuguese Empire. Dutch trade to the Far East increased rapidly.

In 1602, Dutch merchant groups united to form *Vereenigde Oost-Indische Compagnie* (United East-India Company). Backed by the government and well-financed, VOC had the right to establish colonies, make war, manufacture goods, and negotiate treaties like a sovereign state. At the height of its power in the first quarter of the 18th century, VOC dominated one-quarter of the earth, commanded 30,000 employees, and was more powerful than most nations in the world. Unlike other imperial countries, the Dutch lived only by trade. The seven provinces, with a population of 2½ million, had few natural resources. Consequently Dutch efforts were directed to the sea for fish and for trade, and to helping their industrious merchants and financiers.

VOC, efficient and hardworking and ruthless in pursuit of trade, succeeded in dominating commerce in the East. The Company established bases around the rim of the Atlantic for traders, smugglers, and privateers who captured much of the trade flowing from the Americas to Europe.

Joost van der Vondel, Bard of the Dutch East India Company, could sing without self-consciousness:

Wherever profit lead us
To every Sea and Shore
For love of trade and gain
The wide world we'll explore.

Amsterdam became the commercial center of Europe; its warehouses filled with exotic goods from every corner of the world; its harbor teemed with flyboats and East Indiamen. Dutch traders could be found in Russia, the Caribbean, Brazil, Africa, Japan, the Indies... They monopolized trade and supplied the colonies of other nations with goods and slaves. Their well-designed ships, efficient crews, and financial resources made them the carriers of the world.

At its height the Dutch merchant marine controlled the sea and monopolized world trade. Louis XIV's great finance minister Colbert estimated that the Dutch had 15,000 ships out of a world total of 20,000. Little Holland in the 1660's had twice as many vessels as the combined fleets of England, France and Germany.

The Dutch monopolized the Baltic trade which provided them with wood vital for shipbuilding and stores for caulking sailing ships. In the 17th century, when Zaandam became the center of the European timber trade, ships could be built in Holland at half the cost of English construction.

Intrepid Dutch traders of the 17th century founded Archangel on the Arctic Sea in Russia and established strong trading colonies in Moscow and Riga. The Dutch also established the port of Göteborg and for many years controlled the Swedish iron and copper trade, while in the Far East, Japanese copper shipped via Nagasaki, where the Dutch were the only foreign nation allowed to trade, was "the bride for which we dance," to quote Van Imhoff's metaphor of 1745.

In the first half of the 17th century, English and Dutch ships often called at the Cape of Good Hope for refreshment on their way to the East. The Indiamen carried large crews augmented by soldiers. Starvation and scurvy were constant dangers. In 1652, the Dutch took possession of the Cape and excluded competing ships. Therefore, in 1659, the English West India Company established a base on St. Helena. The Dutch captured the island early in 1673, but were in turn defeated by the English later that year and expelled.

England and France began to imitate Dutch trading techniques in the last quarter of the 17th century. They passed laws restricting Dutch traders; the English annexed New Netherlands in 1664 and renamed it New York. Colbert, in France, built up the French merchant marine and excluded Dutch traders from French colonies.

From 1650 to 1697, Holland and England fought three maritime wars which greatly weakened the Dutch. To a nation of only 2½ million people, wars with England and later with France became unsupportable burdens. At first the Dutch held the English at bay. In 1667, Pepys noted in his diary that the Dutch War had broken out again. The daring Dutch fleet sailed up the Thames and burned English ships in the Medbury as far as Chatham while Charles II "amused himself in a moth-hunt in the supper room where his mistresses were feasting in splendor." Pepys gave measurements of two typical Dutch warships: the *White Elephant,* 1482 tons, and the *Golden Lion,* 1477 tons. The former was 131 feet long on the keel, the latter 130 feet. Each had a 46.9 foot beam, drew 19 feet, 8 inches of water and carried three decks.

Weakened by the erosive effects of the later maritime wars of 1672-78 and 1688-97, Holland, by 1700, was a second-class power compared to England and France. She still possessed great wealth and a formidable merchant marine. VOC dividends on capital during the years 1715-1720 were over forty per cent.

The War of the Spanish Succession, begun in 1702, diverted the French from their overseas efforts, weakened Holland and catapulted Britain into her role as a great sea power, and eventually into Mistress of the Seas. In the Lowlands, the Iron Duke of Marlborough won a long series of brilliant military victories, which eventually culminated in the Peace of Utrecht (1711)—a treaty that benefited the traders and merchants of England. Louis XIV was forced to beg for peace and gave up many of France's overseas possessions. In addition, England won Gibraltar and control of the Mediterranean. Henceforth, Holland could play only a relatively minor role in world affairs.

With its new ways of lending money to merchants and shippers, its efficient wooden carrying vessels, its hardworking people, Amsterdam thrived and hundreds of ships from all parts of the world visited its harbor and anchored in the River Y.

Two hundred thousand men and women lived in Amsterdam, making it one of the most populous cities of the 18th century. It was a city carved from the sea and the flat land sticking into the North Sea. The Dutch pushed out the salt water and built four semi-circular canals around the heart of the town. Rows of tree-lined streets, busy quays, and neat brick houses met the traveler's eye, except in the Jordaam district, where the land speculators had put up poorly constructed houses for the immigrants—Jews, *marranos* from Iberia, Huguenots from France, the wretched of all nationalities. The Dutch took them all in; they all contributed to Holland's and Amsterdam's glory and growth.

Like their attitude towards morality, the Dutch Calvinist attitude towards Amsterdam was ambivalent. The great city's wealth was at variance with the strict northern Protestant desire for simplicity and purity. Baruch Spinoza praised the world's wealthiest port:

> *In hac enim florentissima republica et urbe praestantissima omnes cujuscunque nationis et sectae homines summa cum concordia vivunt; et ut alicui bona sua credant, id tantum scire curant, num dives an pauper sit, et num bona fide an dolo solitus sit agere.*

"In this flourishing republic, this city second to none, men of every nation and every sect live together in the utmost harmony; and all they bother to find out, before trusting their goods to anyone, is whether he is rich or poor and whether he is honest or a fraud."

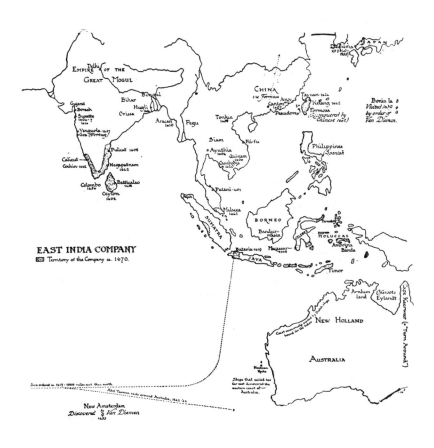

EAST INDIA COMPANY

▨ Territory of the Company ca. 1670.

EMPIRE OF THE GREAT MOGUL

Delhi

CHINA
(via Formosa)

Bonin Is.
Visited in 1650
by order of
Van Diemen.

Bihar
Bengal
Hugli
Orissa

Amoy
Canton
1657
Pescadores

Tayuan 1624
Kelang 1642
Formosa
(conquered by
Chinese 1661)

Gujerat
Broach
Suratte
1608–?
1616

Vengurla 1637
Goa (Portug.)

Aracan
1608

Pegu

Tonkin
1608

Philippines
Spanish

Calicut
Cochin 1662

Pulicat 1608

Negapatnam
1662

Siam

Fai-fu

Ayuthia
1608

Quinam
1636
Cambodia
1620

Colombo
1656

Batticaloa
1638

Ceylon
1602

Patani 1601

Malacca
1641

SUMATRA

BORNEO

Bunder-
massin

Timor

Batavia 1619

Macassar

CELEBES

MOLUCCAS

Amboyna
Banda

JAVA

New Holland

Arnhem
Land

Groote
Eylandt

AUSTRALIA

Houtman
Rocks

Het Rocmar ("Turn Around")

Java ordered in 1617: 1000 miles east then north.

Abel Tasman sails around Australia, 1642–'44.

Coast unaccurately mapped by a Dutch ship
bound for the Indies

Ships that sailed too
far east discovered the
western coast of
Australia.

New Amsterdam
Discovered by Van Diemen
1633

67

But Predikant Bartens, a seventeenth-century Calvinist, looked at Amsterdam's tree-lined streets, its snug shops and red brick houses and found it malevolent:

> *De Hoer aan't Y is voor elk geld te koop*
> *Die vaart voor Paap en Heiden, Moor en Turk,*
> *Die geeft om God noch't lieve Vaderland*
> *Die vraagt naar winst alleen, naar winst! naar winst!*

> "The whore on the Y can be bought with
>   anybody's money;
> She serves Pope and heathen, Moor and Turk,
> She bothers about neither God nor the dear fatherland,
> She is concerned with profit alone, profit alone!
>   Profit alone!"

Contradictions suffused Dutch society, but both its praisers and detractors agreed that trade and wealth built the Calvinist republic.

Amsterdam with ships in the River Y

XII. Batavia

The *Geertruyd,* reached Java in July of 1724.

According to Svilt's journal the ship stayed in that great port for three weeks unloading much of its cargo and taking on other consignments. It then sailed through the Spice Island archipelago and into the China Sea, landing in Fukien and in Japan. Svilt writes:

October 7th, 1724. I spent most of the day on the deck of the *Geertruyd* counting and checking cargo. Batavia is a great port laid out like a Dutch town, but it is peopled by strange men from all corners of the earth. We stayed here for three months, which refreshed the crew greatly. Then we traded with the Tonquinese and Formosans, picking up a variety of goods. Hundreds of ships lie at anchor in the harbor or linger offshore waiting to enter the roads. Alongside our vessel is a Zeelander from Ceylon with three elephants tethered on the aft deck and bags of sweet-smelling cinnamon loaded below and on the fore deck. To port is moored an Arabian dhow loaded to gunwales with dark brown and black precious woods. Our Company vessels bring silk, copper and ivory from Japan,* pepper and cloves from the **Moluccas** and a thousand other products from our factories throughout the East. The goods are stored in Company warehouses and factories, and then loaded onto ships bound for Holland or other ports controlled by the Company.

October 8th. After prayers, this morning I set out to find Piek Houtman. Batavia's streets were filled with Chinese merchants, who have set up little shops wherever there is an empty spot. They sell goods from Canton and, indeed, goods from the Company's stores (which is against regulations). But private trade is rife. Though many have come here empty handed, Chinese merchants have grown rich through their ceaseless industry. I ascertained that they have an excellent reputation as being honest traders but poor soldiers when the Company calls on them to fight. Indeed, he said, they are always running in the same direction as the enemy: they flee when he attacks and they bravely advance when he flies.

Besides the Chinese, a hundred other nations, many decked in fantastic garb, walk the broad, clean streets of the Dutch town. It is a law that only Christians can dress like Dutchmen: all nonbelievers must wear their native costumes. I have seen Moluccans, Arabs, Balinese, Cambojans, Callicut merchants, Amboinese and Ceylonese

---

*In the 16th century, over 200,000 Japanese had adopted Christianity, mainly through the efforts of Spanish and Portuguese missionaries. But in the last part of the 17th century, the Shogun considered Christians subversive and a threat to his authority; he killed or forcibly converted most of the others. In 1637 thirty thousand Catholics held out on the Shimoburo Peninsula, where the Shogun's troops could not reach them. He asked the Dutch for help. Dutch ships and cannon aided the Shogun. In return for their assistance in exterminating their coreligionists, he gave the East India Company exclusive trading rights in Japan. The Dutch monopolized Japanese trade for over 200 years.

Ships in the Batavia roadstead, 1649

slaves, Europeans, Portuguese, English, and Danes. Today I saw a dark Mardijker, a half-Christian Indian, dressed like a quack's monkey at a country fair with a European shirt and trousers but no shoes. They have a reputation for shrewdness.

Many of the women deck themselves in exotic and strange costumes trimmed with silk and gold and jewels. The richer women never go abroad on the streets without a convoy of slaves, whom they abuse shamelessly. Most of these women, though married to rich Dutchmen, have little that is European about them. They speak a bastard Portuguese dialect and behave like heathens. One fat Malay woman, who passed me in the street, grew angry at her slave girl, who followed her in the street holding a *pajang* over her head to shield it from the sun. The rich woman knocked the poor slave girl to the ground and lashed her with a whip, all the time cursing her in Portuguese, the common language of most of the dissolute women whom our Dutchmen have taken to wife. The women never learn to speak Dutch properly and pass their bad habits onto their children. Batavia is no place to properly raise a Dutch child.

Near the massive Casteel which guards the entrance to Batavia, I saw Governor General Durven carried on a chair held up in the air by four black slaves. He was escorted by a company of dragoons and halberdiers. All passers-by must stop whatever they are doing and bow respectfully as his gilded carriage passes. In his carriage, I spied two young and beautiful dark girls. The tavernkeeper, Meyer, told me that the Governor spends his evenings with many different females and has a harem that rivals Solomon's. Batavia is a wicked city.

Voluptuous and lascivious women openly walk the

streets, especially in the quarter frequented by the mariners. The Bugenese women are deemed especially desirable by those lost men who have given up all semblance of respectability, as have many of our countrymen who have lived here for years.

Piek Houtman and I ate and drank together at Meyer's tavern last night. Though all taverns must be closed by 9 P.M., there is no shortage of wine and beer after that hour and the streets are full of drunken men and women till the sun rises.

Piek regaled me with unseemly stories of his and his companions' encounters with slave women. I listened politely, though much of what he told me filled me with abhorrence. There is little morality in Batavia; drinking and fornicating are the order of the day among the Europeans. I am particularly saddened to see how low my friend has fallen from the Christian teachings he held so devoutly when he sailed to Batavia ten years ago. I hardly recognize him. His body has grown fat; and his soul, I am afraid, has grown quite foul.

Piek brought me to his home and introduced me to his young wife who is a Mardijker and nominally a Christian. I was surprised to see Piek's wife sit on her haunches and eat her curry with her fingers like an Asiatic savage, but Piek assures me that it is the custom in Batavia. She spoke a strange medley of Portuguese, Indian, and Dutch. He introduced me to a young boy named Bandino Franz, who, he said, was his "nephew," though others have told me the relationship is closer. Bandino is 15 but he looks younger. He is a pretty and well-mannered lad. Piek asked me to take Bandino with me to Holland and to educate him, as the climate in Batavia was unhealthy and the schools turn out only ignorant louts. I agreed to do this for him.

Bandino is a slight, strangely beautiful boy with the skin and eyelashes of a Javanese Houri, tinged with wisps of blond hair. He moves his small, delicate hands and feet with great deliberation. He is thin, spry, and well-proportioned.

He speaks slowly in poor Dutch, giving one the initial impression that he is a boor; yet he is fluent in the bastard Portuguese spoken here by the women and the slaves, and he can recite Indian and Arabic poetry. Piek and I were discussing our own youth and some of the women we had known when we were young together. Bandino sat quietly listening. A slave girl brought in a pitcher of wine. Bandino rose, bowed to us, smiled and said: "Love is the water, if not the wine of life..." He smiled at me and walked out of the room. Piek feels that he is peculiar, and will only grow worse if he stays in Batavia.

When walking in the lush garden with me, Bandino recited strange and moving poetry of a mad Indian Sufi named Sarmad, who went naked through the streets of Delhi. The Mogul's son loved Sarmad, and the Mogul had him murdered. His poetry is most moving.

XIII. Ascension. Svilt Moves to a Cave.

June 21st. In the morning I lifted up my hands to heaven, offered my prayers, and went to my flag. On the way I looked for food to assuage my raging hunger, but found none. The hand of Providence is withdrawn. Grief and care oppressed my anxious soul. My senses were overwhelmed in depth of thought and every moment threatened my destruction. What pangs, alas! do wretched mortals feel who headstrong tread the giddy passes of life and leave the beauteous paths of righteousness, pleased to increase the number of the damned. Ate salted fowls.

On the 22nd, my water being expended, I took my buckets to fetch more water to my tent, which I could not accomplish till the day was far spent, being forced to travel in great misery over the rocks, rocks so sharp that they cut my bare feet.

The 23rd I spent my time in prayer. When not praying I looked out upon the sea for ships, and from the 24th to the 27th incessantly continued my prayers.

On the 28th, in the morning, I went to see whether my flag was standing, and after having humbled myself before

God and desired his mercy and forgiveness I returned to my tent, took my bedding and some other necessaries and went to the middle of the island, where I fixed a new habitation in the cavity of a rock, it being much nearer the rivulet of water before mentioned. But, to my great dismay, when I went to get some there was not one drop! I fetched a few eggs; some were speckled like those of our Holland birds. I boiled them in my teakettle with some of the water I had left, then went to the south side of the island, where there is a large hill of sand and rocks, upon which I found more purslane, which I gathered and put into my sack, together with some eggs. I fried both and eat them with a good appetite but was obliged to return lest I should become lost in the dark and not be able to find my new abode. Before I arrived at the rock I was almost dead for want of drink, and my skin was blistered in a terrible manner with the scorching heat of the sun, so that it was ready to peel from my flesh.

On the 29th I went to the top of the hill to look out for shipping. Afterwards, walking on the seashore, I perceived a piece of wood sinking in the sand. At first I took it for a tree but, coming nearer, I found it to be a cross. I embraced it in my arms and prayed fervently to God to deliver me. I believe there had been a man buried there belonging to some ship. In my return to my cave my feet were miserably cut with the sharp stones, that I had liked to have perished in coming down the hill. When I had got to my tent I rested and then went out again and in my walk found a piece of glass bottle. With this I descended into a deep pit and scooped some water of brackish taste, so that my search proved of no effect. As I was returning to my cave in a disconsolate manner, bemoaning my wretched fate, I found some scattered wood, which I made up into a bundle and carried with me. I was no sooner come to my cavern but I heard a dreadful noise, resembling many coppersmiths at work. The din stopped as suddenly as it had begun. After saying my prayers I went **again to get some greens and eggs, which I** drank the last of the water I had left.

On the 30th I went in search of water but could find none. Now all hopes were lost. That evening I saw a skeleton appear near my tent with his hand uplifted, **Strange to relate, I was not afraid.**

The following two chapters are from Svilt's journal before he landed on Ascension. *Capetown, Homeward Bound* deals with his experience with Bandino in "The Tavern of the Seven Seas." This is followed by an account of a curious sermon preached aboard the *Geertruyd* by Predikant Flugal.

VI. Capetown: Homeward Bound

March 2nd, 1725. Our storm-lashed fleet, minus one vessel sunk in a gale off Madagascar, touched at Capetown. Our trip from Molucca had been marred by an attack of French pirates and by severe storms. We must stop at the Cape to repair our mizzen mast, take on new sails and provision the ship. I am mightily glad to be here alive.

My shipmates too were pleased to be in port; they roared ashore like storm waves hitting a rocky coast.

Bandino accompanied me around the pretty town. It was his first visit, and I felt obliged to protect him as best I could from the many dangerous vices in this port. We first bought red shirts fabricated in the Company's factory in Cormandel. Bandino's dark skin goes very well with red. We bought bright silks from Bengal and some curious statues made of bronze for our private trade..

Sunday we went to the small Calvinist church near the wharf to hear an old Predikant preach of hell and damnation for sinners, a sermon that seemed to affect

Bandino greatly. Then we joined in singing a mournfully
affecting cantata which reminded us that we all must die:

> *Set their house in order*
> *For thou shalt die*
> *and not live...*
> *The old Covenant holds:*
> *Man, thou art born to die!*
> *Yes, so come to me Lord Jesus.*

Against the harbour near where lives the Governor, the
Company slaves and servants have built a strong fort
facing the sea. Inland, some three hundred paces westward
of the fort, is the main town with some fifty or sixty
houses -mostly low dwellings, but solidly built of Holland
brick with stone walls around.

Towards the mountains on the backside of the town, the
Company has erected a large, stone house walled about
with a high stone wall that surrounds a large, well-stocked
garden. I walked in the garden with Bandino to view the
divers, herbs, flowers, roots and fruits planted therein.
Hand in hand, we walked along curious gravel paths and
arbors. The plants are watered by a brook that descends
out of a mountain nearby. The brook is cut into many
channels and thus conveys life-giving water to all parts of
the garden. Thick hedges more than nine feet tall line the
walks. Paths and trees, and indeed all the varied plants
herein, are kept exceedingly neat by the Company's slaves.

A great number of Indian and Negro slaves brought
from all parts of the Company's possessions care for the
garden. We saw many of them at work, weeding, pruning,
trimming and mulching the plants and trees.

The Company allows all strangers to walk in their
garden, but none are allowed to pick fruit except with
permission of the Company's servants. While Bandino and

I were in the pomegranate grove, we spied a rash English bosun, clandestinely pull a handful of fruit from the grove. He was caught in the act by big black slaves, who threatened to carry him before the Governor. It cost the bosun some money to make his peace.

After we had dallied in the garden, we headed for the docks where the *Geertruyd* was moored. We came upon four of our shipmates standing in line outside the Company's slave lodge waiting their turn to fornicate with the colored slave whores. A comely dark-skinned wench leaned out of a window in the lodge and threw a piece of sugar cane at Bandino to attract his attention. She smiled and motioned for us to join her, an action which made Bandino turn his pretty head away in distress. The crewmen standing in line, many of whom were drunk though it was the Sabbath, mocked at us when we refused to join them in line.

Nicholas Fockema shouted at us, "What's the matter boys, no balls? Do you squat to piss?"

Another laughed at us and said, "Slave cunt not good enough for you? Come on in, you'll find it smells the same as what you're used to..." They threw at us other offensive jibes which made me angry. But I held in my anger, for I had had words with some of these louts before and knew no good would come of arguing with them.

Near us stood an elderly Moslem, from Persia I believe, who had been watching while our shipmates taunted us. Before we could leave the scene he came up to us and asked if Bandino was a Christian or a Moslem. I told him that his mother had been a Moslem but had died young. He pointed at the sailors swaying in line waiting for the whores, and said:

"You Dutch Christians preach to us of your superior

Tavern in Dorp Street, Capetown, 1717

religion. The Calvinists are, to hear them, the salt of the earth with God-given morals.'' He pointed to the line of drunken sailors ''Look at how you really are. You behave like swine, like drunken, whoring pigs. I would never allow my daughter to marry a Dutchman. I would break her neck first. Now you have the better ships, the bigger guns, and you make us your slaves. But one day Allah will be revenged.'' I could not reply. The old man walked away. Bandino, whose mother had been a Bugenese slave and a Moslem, was much upset by the old man's harangue—Oh Christ, how different is your ideal world from the vile existence that surrounds me and my shipmates?

That evening aboard our ship, little Bandino asked me to read to him a portion of the Bible which touched on the punishment for sinners who do not tread the narrow path of righteousness. I read him a sermon by St. Paul, which we both took to heart.

XV. Predikant Flugal Preaches a Sermon
(Excerpt from Svilt's journal before he landed on Ascension)

April 20th, 1725: towards sundown I was standing amid ships to port, watching the sun sink toward Brazil and smoking my pipe. Bandino and Micael Lucas, an English deck hand, stood nearby, Micael with a mug of grog and Bandino with a sweet smile, when Predikant Flugal strode out from the officer's castle followed by his *Kranktrooster*, Boom Spiegel.

Lucas, who is an Anglican, but not a very devout Christian, whispered to me, "Here comes a fat drunk followed by a skinny idiot. We are in for the evening's entertainment."

Flugal seemed to sway as if he had had too much gin. Spiegel rang the ship's bronze bell to call all hands to the main deck for the service. Usually this was a short affair led by Spiegel at which we would sing a few hymns. Lucas did not like Predikants.

"It is bad enough that these lazy louts eat the best food, drink gin with the officers and do no work. But on top of that the hypocrites preach to us about our sins. What rot!"

I said, "Flugal is a very learned divine."

"Why? Because he can spout verbatim whole pages of the Bible like an elephant pissing? He drinks and whores like the rest of us. I saw him sneaking out of the slave lodge in Capetown."

With the ringing of the bell the crew assembled slowly from different parts of the ship, many of the men carrying their rations of grog in pewter mugs. Flugal did not seem to mind their drinking. The sailors gathered on the main deck while Flugal stood above us on the poop deck. He sent his *Kranktrooster* below to rout out the whole crew. It was clear that he had a long sermon in store for us. We noticed that he swayed more than the motion of our ship, which rode steadily before a small breeze, would warrant.

Lucas said, "The fat slob is soused again; we're in for a long blast of hot air. Lord preserve us!"

Flugal cleared his throat, glared down at us below, and, so it seemed to me, looked at me in particular.

"We men are weak vessels," he began. "All of us sin. 'Know ye not that the unrighteous shall not inherit the kingdom of God. Be not deceived: neither fornicators, nor idolators, nor adulterers, nor effeminate, nor abusers of themselves with mankind,' said St. Paul to the Corinthians. 'Meat for the belly, and the belly for meats, but God shall destroy both...Now the body is not for fornication, but for the Lord...' Some sins God forgives. Some bring down His full wrath, not only on the sinner, but also on his companions! Let us sing the hymn 'God He Is Strong.'"

Whilst we sang, I felt that the Predikant's eyes were on me. He had come upon me earlier in the day while I was going over the cargo list. He had asked to see the ship's bill of lading. He became quite angry when I refused to show it to him without the Captain's permission.

In his booming voice, the Predikant continued:

"Foremost among the wicked crimes accursed to the Lord are crimes against nature—unnatural acts performed by vile and degenerate men. I refer to the sins of Sodom and Gomorrah. 'Know ye not that your body is the temple of the Holy Ghost which is in you...?' " Here Lucas whispered in my ear: "Our bodies may belong to the Holy Ghost, but our souls belong to the VOC." This made me smile, but I confess, I did not relish the Predikant's sermon.

"Recall, sinners, that when Josiah was ordered by God to purify his Chosen People, 'Josiah did brake down the houses of the Sodomites' (II Kings 23.7). The Lord cannot abide men who commit such evil.

" 'The men of Sodom were wicked and sinners before the Lord, exceedingly.' Note the word 'exceedingly.' And 'the Lord said, Because the cry of Sodom and Gomorrah is great and because their sin is very grievous, I will destroy them' (Genesis 18 20). What was their sin? When Lot had given refuge in his house to two strangers, the men of Sodom came to his door and cried to him, 'Where are these men? Bring them out unto us that we may bugger them.'

"But Lot was a righteous man and he answered, 'Behold now, I have two daughters which have not known men. Let me, I pray, bring them out unto you and do ye to them as is good unto your eyes; only unto these men do nothing...' But the unnatural men of Sodom were evil and would not harken unto Lot. Thereupon the Lord became angry and he told Lot and his family to leave the evil city when the sun next rose over the earth. 'Then the Lord rained upon Sodom and upon Gomorrah brimstone and fire from out of heaven... And he destroyed those cities and all the plains, and all the inhabitants of the cities, and that which grows upon the ground' (Genesis 19:24). So saith the holy Bible.

"To avoid a fate like unto that which overtook Sodom, to preserve our fleet and our lives and our cargoes, we must root out from our midst all unnatural evil, all abusers of mankind. If we fail to do so the Lord will surely rain fire and brimstone on our ships. We are at His tender mercy. 'Keep my commandments and live-bind them upon thy finger, write them upon the table of thine heart' (Prov.7.2). Now let us sing another hymn. Spiegel will lead you...

XVI. Ascension. Svilt's Water Dries Up.
He Sights a Flock of Goats.

July the 1st. The water being dried up in every place
where I was used to get it, I was ready to perish with
thirst, therefore offered up my prayers to God to deliver
and preserve me as he did Moses and the children of Israel,
by causing the water to gush out of the rock; esteeming
their sufferings not to equal mine, seeing that I was not
only bereft of food and raiment but banished from all
human society and left to be devoured by the birds of
prey, who infest this desolate island. Whilst I was rambling
up and down in quest, ascending the top of a hill, I espied
a herd of goats* a-grazing at a distance, which I chased

---

*Early explorers often left goats and pigs on newly discovered islands in the
expectation that the animals would breed and thus provide them with a
supply of meat when next their ship touched that coast. This practice
often resulted in destroying the native ecosystem of many islands which
were fragile to begin with. The goats often multiplied to the point where
they denuded many small islands of vegetation.

with all the speed I was able, but to my sorrow found they were too swift for me. I still followed them at a distance, in hopes of finding the place where they watered, when, after a long pursuit, I came to a pit five or six fathom deep, which I descended, but found no water. I believe by the goats' frequenting it there is sometimes water, chiefly occasioned by the fall of rain. It is a miracle to me how the goats keep themselves alive in a dry season, since water is so scarce throughout the whole island. I should long before this have perished had it not been for a gallon of water that I had before preserved, with a full resolution not to make use of it unless compelled by dire necessity.

I afterwards went to the strand but could discover nothing that would be of any service to me. I then proceeded farther up the island and, having ascended a lofty hill, espied a great herd of goats, with their kids accompanying them, which I pursued with the like ill success. As there are so many on the island it is surprising I had not discovered them sooner, but believe they give their young ones suck in the holes of the rocks, till the sun has drawn the moisture thence, then sally out abroad in search of more. Here I found about two gallons of water more in a rock.

July the 4th I moved my things from my cave and went to the west side of the island to settle my abode, being sure there was no water on this side. I prayed to God to send a plenteous rain. The 5th to the 8th I prayed and looked for water.

On the 9th, as I was walking pensively on the sand, half dead with thirst, I heard a dismal noise of cursing and swearing in my own language, during which time a cloud of birds obscured the light of the sun.

On the 10th I ascended another steep hill but found nothing but a piece of wood, which I took with me to prop my new habitation.

From the 11th to the 18th nothing remarkable happened.

On the 19th I went out in search of water but found none. I found some birds' eggs and brought them home to eat, using my water very sparingly, which lasted me only the next day.

From the 21st to the 31st, the sun beat down from a merciless sky. I rationed myself to a mug of water a day, which I would sip slowly and give thanks to God for his mercy. Tongue cannot express, nor thought devise, the wretched torments I endured. My mouth is continually parched, my tongue is cracked, my skin has become withered like old leather.

XVII. Ascension. Svilt Encounters Swarms of Rats. He Is Reduced to Drinking His Own Urine.

From the 1st to the 3rd of August I walked out with my bucket and found a little water which the goats had left in the hollow of a rock. This rejoiced me very much. I rolled my cask there and scooped it all out as clean as I could and I carried it to my tent.

On the 4th I walked along the strand and found a broken oar and three or four small pieces of wood, which was very acceptable. Proceeding a little further, I espied something which appeared to me at a distance like a house and, calling to mind that I had heard the Portuguese formerly inhabited this island, made all the haste possible thither, and to my great surprise found it to be a white hollow rock, in the cavity of which were some nails and broken glass bottles. These were but of little use to me; therefore I took my wood and marched home.

On the 5th I went abroad again to seek for food but returned overwhelmed with grief and want.

The 6th I went to my tent on the beach and observed

that three or four of the pease and calwaines which I had before set in the ground were coming up. I had watered them with my urine. But upon a strict inquiry I found the vermin had devoured all the rest, which damped my former joy.

The 7th. There has not been an hour's rain for the space of three months, neither is there one drop of water to be found on the whole island except what I have preserved in my cask; and if God Almighty of his great goodness does not speedily refresh the earth with a plentiful rain, I must inevitably perish.

From the 8th to the 10th I searched carefully but could find no water, therefore endeavored to prepare myself for that great and terrible change which I was convinced was near at hand, begging for salvation through the merits of my blessed Lord and Savior Jesus Christ, who shall change our vile bodies and make them like unto His.

On the 11th I went to my tent on the strand, where I again heard a terrible metal-beating noise but could not tell from whence it proceeded. I resolved to go up the hill to endeavor to inform myself, but saw nothing there but a cloud of birds (of which mention has been made before) and am therefore fully persuaded the noise was made by them. It was a great satisfaction to me only to think I was so deceived.

From the 12th to the 17th I went about every part of the island but to my great concern I could find no water. I gauged my cask. I had not now above six gallons left, which made me boil nothing and drink but little.

On the 18th and 19th the same; but, being near sunset, and I a great distance from my tent on the contrary side of the island, I lost my way; so was compelled to lie all night between two rocks; where I was disturbed with so great a number of rats that I was afraid of being devoured by them. I have always loathed rats and I heartily wished myself on the strand again.

The 20th: I prayed incessantly to Almighty God to send rain, then took my spade and dug two fathoms, but found no moisture. I viewed the motions of the heaven, in hopes to see some friendly cloud o'ercharged with water, that might disgorge itself upon the barren rocks and grant relief to me in this distress, but my hopes were vain. Then I wildly wandered over the sterile hills and begged the rocks and sands might cover me, deeming the goats that browsed about the island far happier than that man whose affection had been the occasion of his suffering.

On the 21st I went rambling about the island with my scoop in hand but found no refreshment. The small quantity of water I had left being almost exhausted, I was forced to make water in my scoop and drank my urine, thinking it better than salt water. I was so extremely thirsty that my lips stuck together.

With the sinking of the sun my body cooled and I felt much relieved. In the dim light I copied from my hymn book a prayer that gave me consolation:

Christ will not fail me;
As the true witness declares with fearsome explosion
and with great bursts of noise
the mountains collapse.
My Savior will not deceive me:
My Father must love me,
In Jesus' red blood my name is inscribed;
He protects me yet!

If I should be hurled into the sea,
The Lord who still lives on the mighty waters,
The Lord who has granted me my very life,

Will protect me. The sea monsters
    will not swallow me.
Though the great waves toss me, grip me,
    and in their rage
Try to pull me down to the deep,
I know it is my Father testing me,
And I will think on Jonah.
Like Peter, I will give the Lord my soul.
He wants me strong in faith;
He wants to watch my fearful soul, which,
Poor thing, ever wavers and weakens.
In his goodness he wants me to stand fast.
Upon this rock must my foot be firmly planted
    until the end.
If I stand firm in rockbound faith,
His hand will know it when
    He reaches down from heaven
At the moment of great joy and death
To raise me up again.

XVIII. Explication: The Climate and Currents Surrounding Ascension
Reflections on the Drinking of Urine.

Ascension lies in the trade-wind belt. It has a mean temperature of 85°F on the coast and 75°F at an elevation of 2000 feet. In the 19th century the British regarded it highly for its health-giving climate.

A vacationer from Northern Europe, would no doubt find the climate of Ascension Island delightful. It is dry, free of pollen, and warm. The island lies just south of the equatorial current and in the midst of the weak South Atlantic gyre. These currents shift north during the European summer and south during the European winter. Most of the year Ascension lies in a high pressure zone of clear skies and gentle westerly breezes which carry little moisture and rarely drop any rain. In the lowlands part of the island, rainfall averages 5 inches a year. The higher peaks capture a bit more moisture, which tinges them green.

The unlucky Svilt, had he landed on Ascension during the months of March and April, when cloudbursts dump heavy rains on the higher parts of the island, might have had an easier time of it. Or if he had landed on an island 10° north or south of Ascension, his chances for survival would have improved.

Ascension is today a British possession. It is inhabited mainly by personnel who maintain the underwater cables used for transmission of telephone information. The inhabitants get most of their water from a spring in what is called Breakneck Valley, located in a fairly inaccessible part of the island facing to the southwest. Bamboo and other plants have been introduced on the slopes of Green Mountain. These plants are able to extract some moisture from the clouds and fog passing over the island.

During the Second World War the United States stationed a squadron of airplanes on Ascension. Because of the great distance of the island from sources of supply, a rather elaborate aquaponics farm was established to grow fresh vegetables. This project successfully produced tomatoes, lettuce and other salad greens.

The Air Force was at first troubled by the great hordes of birds which nest on the island. Severe measures had to be taken to protect the airplanes from disaster caused by catching birds in the planes' propellers.

The American Air Force aviators used to sing a little ditty:

"If you don't find Ascension
Your wife will get a pension."

Directly parallel to Ascension, the nearest landfall eastward is the Congo Coast. Westward of Ascension lies the Bulge of Brazil, which has hot wet summers and hot dry winters. The land around Recife has been plagued by unreliable rainfall and drought for centuries.

In January the Doldrum belt extends to about 50⁰ S in the Atlantic, bringing some moisture, but through most of the year the doldrum belt shifts north and is replaced by the trade winds and the calm, clear horse latitudes—sunny days, clear nights—little rain.

While Svilt's drinking of urine may seem strange to us today, in dry climates and during droughts humans have often drunk urine. Human urine has a lower salt content than sea water. Fresh urine is best; 17th-and 18th-century mariners report that after drinking their own urine a number of times after it had been through the gut, the liquid turned red.

History records that men and women have been forced to drink urine on many unhappy occasions. The Bible cites at least three examples when people under seige or during a drought drank urine. See, for example, II Kings 18.27, Isaiah 36.2 and Ezekiel 4.12-15.

Long sieges, which cut off the drinking water of cities, forced the inhabitants of Jerusalem, and more recently Ghent, to drink urine. During the famine of Louis XIV's reign, many peasants were reduced to drinking urine. The inhabitants of arid regions still resort to it in times of need.

J.G. Bourke, in "Scatalogical Rites of All Nations," cites numerous examples of shipwrecked and castaway sailors and soldiers who drank their own urine.

A few Asian tribes drink the urine of others who have eaten hallucinatory mushrooms in order to again fall under the influence of the excreted chemical. But they do it for stimulation rather than necessity.

XIX. Ascension. No Rain.

On the 22nd I took a walk (after having offered up my sacrifice of prayer) on the strand, where I found a turtle,* which I killed, and drank near a gallon of the blood instead of water, and took some of the fat and eggs and fried them together and eat them. But the blood did not agree with me, neither did it quench my raging thirst, so that I was forced to drink a large quantity of my urine.

On the 23rd, having no hopes of finding any more water, I took some of the turtle blood, which I had killed the day before, after letting it settle all night, which I mixed with my own urine and boiled some tea in it, and

---

*Sea turtles swim ashore, mainly during the months of December through May, to lay their eggs in the sandy beaches. The female turtle will deposit from 100 to 200 eggs in a hole laboriously dredged in the sand with her clumsy flippers. The hole may be up to two feet deep. Once the eggs are deposited, the turtle covers them with sand and quickly waddles back into the sea. Warmed by the sun, the eggs hatch in about a month. The young hatchlings immediately crawl down the strand into the water. On shore, sea turtles and their eggs are extremely vulnerable to predatory birds and to man. Sailing ships often put into Ascension to turn turtles; some weighed 600 to 800 pounds.

thought it far preferable to raw blood. About four in the afternoon I returned to my tent, having nothing to drink but turtle blood, but presently was taken so violently with the flux, occasioned by the drinking it, that I could hardly stand. This was rather a satisfaction to me than a shock, hoping the sooner to end my miserable days, desiring nothing more. I with great difficulty got to my tent.

From the 24th to the 27th I had no thought of anything but death, continuing very ill, but prayed earnestly that God would put an end to my misery. The fowl's eggs no way relieving my thirst, I was therefore forced to boil me some more tea in my urine and settled blood, there being plenty of the turtles on the island.

On the 28th at three in the morning I went out and killed one turtle with my hatchet and put the blood in my bucket. There was a great quantity of water in the bladder which I drank, it being much better than the blood, but it did not continue long upon my stomach. I then cut off some of the flesh and carried it to my tent. And, being very dry, I boiled some more tea in the turtle blood, but my stomach, being weak, required greater nourishment; and the blood, being bitter, proved a strong emetic and I could no longer retain it.

On the 29th I could not sleep, occasioned by a drought and dizziness in my head, which afflicted me to that degree that I though I should have run mad. I once more went to search for water but found none.

On the 30th I prayed to be dissolved and be with Christ, for most part of the day thinking my sufferings exceeded that of Job, I being debarred the pleasure of human conversation, sick and had no clothing; my actions unjustifiable, my torments inexpressible and my destruction unavoidable. I tried to compose myself after I had prayed to the Almighty for rain or that I might die before morning. In the afternoon I endeavored to get out of my tent but could not walk, I was so weak; therefore dressed some turtle eggs. I had some turtle flesh in my tent but it stank, but was in such agony for want of water that tongue can't express. I caught three boobies and drank the blood of them.

My brain is dizzy; I know not what I did.

XX. Protestant Morality and Attitudes Towards Death in the First Half of the XVIII Century

While Svilt was languishing on Ascension in the year 1725, J. S. Bach wrote a Recitative and Aria for Anna Magdalena Bach. These two reformation songs catch the mournful religious tone of the times, when sweet death was welcome to sinners.

Recitative:

> *It is enough for me:*
> *my comfort is this, this only,*
> *That Jesus may please to be mine, and I His.*
> *I have Him now by faith, since I see already,*
> *Like Simeon, the joy of that life.*
> *Let us go with that man! Oh, that the Lord*
> *Would free me from the chains of my body!*
> *Even if it were not time to leave you, World,*
> *I would say joyfully "I have had enough."*

Aria:

> *Sleep, you tired eyes. Fall gently, joyfully asleep.*
> *I have no share in you, World,*
> *   which could serve my soul.*
> *I shall stay here no longer. Here I heap up woe;*
> *There I shall see sweet peace and silent rest.*

(Recitative: "Ich habe genug"; and
 Aria: "Schlummert ein.")

A popular book on philosophy by the Englishman David Hartley, published in 1749, gives an insight into the moral attitudes of certain Protestants of Svilt's era.

"When impure Desires are allowed, indulged and heightened voluntarily...they will draw to themselves all the other Pleasures of our Nature, and even...convert them into Incentives and Temptations. So that all the Desires, Designs and Ideas of such Persons are tainted with Lust...But impure Desires subsist, like vicious ones of other Kinds, long after the Pains outweigh the Pleasures...

"...impure and vicious Desires indulged in and heightened voluntarily must not only end frequently in Indifference, but even in Hatred and Abhorrence...

"Avoid gross corporeal Gratification. Every person who desires true charity and purity of Heart must be watchful over his Thoughts, his Discourses, his Studies and his Intercourses with the World in general and with the other Sex in particular. There is no security but in flight, in turning our minds from the associated Circumstances and begetting a new Train of Thoughts and Desires, by an honest, virtuous, religious Attention to the Duty of the Time and Place. To which must be added great Abstinence in Diet and bodily Labour."

Yet in England, Tom Jones was lollygagging about caring not a whit for stern morality.

Medieval cruelty still infused everyday life; every Dutch town had its torture chamber. Even women and boys were often branded with red-hot irons when caught thieving. Whippings were common. In 1703 a man who tried to sabotage a Freisian dike was broken at the wheel at Amsterdam. In spite of Amstedam's toleration of different religious sects, blasphemy was a crime: Adrien Koerbagh, a lawyer and physician, was sentenced to ten years in prison, ten years of exile plus a fine of 4000 gulders for publishing "Godless and God-Mocking Books"; his prosecutor had asked for a sentence of thirty years in prison, confiscation of all Koerbagh's property and that his right thumb be cut off and his tongue pierced with a red hot bodkin.

ESAJAS VAN DE VELDE: *The Gallows*. Etching

XXI. Ascension. Svilt Recalls the Execution of a Boy Thief.

August 30th. The bright sun and lack of water; the solitude; the continually crying terns in the sky; the bleak landscape—I fear I will lose my senses completely. Christ preserve me. Today, when looking at the sea for ships that do not come, strange memories swam into my head. I recalled an event that occurred when I was a boy. I have not thought of it for twenty-five years.

When I was twelve, my guardian took me with him to the main square in Delft to watch the execution of a boy who had stolen a goose. The boy was about my age and thin and dirty. He stood with head bowed on a platform which held twelve gibbets, from one of which hung an old man. The boy's left hand had been chopped off; he held a dirty rag against the stump to stanch the bleeding. His eyes were closed. His thin legs were tightly closed in pain.

We stood with a crowd of half drunken burghers and workmen who had come to see the hanging. Some of them were eating bread and cheese and sausages and drinking beer. A fat Predikant climbed to the platform next to the skinny boy. He moved his fat hands. After he had silenced the crowd, he said, "This miserable boy has stolen property and under the laws of God and the Republic of Holland he must be punished for it. For if we encourage theft by not dealing with it severely, others will turn to stealing instead of to honest work to fill their needs. Property is sacred." He looked at the boy and said, "God bless his soul."

When the Predikant descended, a black-hooded hangman climbed up to where the boy was tied. The boy was too frightened to open his eyes. But I remember that he cried out, "We were hungry. My mother is starving..."

The hangman put the noose around the boy's neck and kicked open the trap door beneath his thin body. The boy screamed once, but the rope soon silenced him and his little body swung quietly in the breeze.

In the crowd standing next to me was a big, rough man whose face had been branded with a hot iron and whose ear had been chopped off. He said, "That kid tried to steal the wrong goose. He should leave the burgomaster's property alone...See this, I was branded by a hot iron by the good people in Leyden and my ear was chopped off because I took a loaf of bread from a baker...better than being hanged on a black gibbet or broken on the wheel."

I asked, "How can the hangman in good conscience murder such a young boy?"

The mutilated man replied, "I would do it, too. He gets three guilders per head, and nine guilders more if he buries the corpse...When I was a seaman on the *Zeeland*, I got 10 guilders a month. That hangman killed over two hundred thieves last year. He is a rich man." He held up his right hand, which had a smooth scar on its palm. "See that, sonny? The mate of the *Zeeland* caught me taking a shirt from a seaman's chest. No matter the man had died of scurvy and been thrown overboard. The mate had my hand nailed to the mast. I stayed there like Christ for two days 'til I pulled my hand free. Calvinist justice! Phagh!'' The man spat at the gibbet; he must have been a Catholic.

I see the boy swinging in the breeze as if it happened yesterday. Perhaps God put the memory before me to tell me that my end is near.

XXII. Ascension

On the 31st as I was crawling on the sand, for I could not walk three steps, I espied a turtle and, being so weak that I could not carry my buckets, I cut off his head with my hatchet, then laid myself on my side and sucked the blood as it ran out; afterwards put my arm into the body and plucked his bladder out, which I crawled away with to my tent, and put the water into a teakettle; then returned back and cut it up, in order to get the eggs, in doing of which the helve of my hatchet broke. This was still an addition to my misfortunes; but I got out some of the eggs, carried them to my tent and fried them, then boiled me some tea in my own urine, which was very nauseous to me but revived me very much.

Why do I continue to write when I can hardly hold a pen in my dried-out fingers, which are almost as thin as my quill? What else is there to do but pray and write. In a few days I must surely die. Only a miracle can save me. My life evaporates with every drop of water that leaves my withered body.

Water. So common and single a substance. It is a constant menace to the dikes of my homeland. I am surrounded by a sea of it; yet I die for lack of it. Today, I dreamed I was back again on the *Geertruyd*, drinking my daily ration of schnapps and water. Then I dreamed I was sitting with Piek Houtman drinking great steins of beer in Meyer's Tavern near the quay in Batavia. Then I had visions of roast ducklings and quince served to me with white bread by my wife, all washed down with Portuguese wine. 300 casks of wine from Capetown and water lie in the hold of the fat *Geertruyd*, presided over by the great Red Lion figurehead at her bow and protected by 200 soldiers and 38 guns. Her green poop is wonderfully gilded and decorated with the Red Lion of Zeeland. When she flew her 40 flags and pennants, who could not be proud of her—despite her bedbugs which ate me alive, and the fat rats that crawled up the bulkheads and over my hammock slung between two gun, barrel mounts 'tween decks. My eyes never failed to light up at the sight of the red, white and blue flag flying over her ornate castle.

The empty pewter mug on the floor of my cave bears the mark "VOC," as does every other item on the Company's ships. My employers say: "Christ is good, but trade is better." My kindly executioners. How many other of the Company's 30,000 servants practice the stupid sins, if sins they be, of which I was accused? Dear Jesus, I am innocent, am I not? The heavens are full of angelic men who look like women. Christ, my savior, should loving and giving pleasure to brothers be sinful? Was it wrong to comfort Bandino?

Meeting of the High Seventeen

XXIII. Meeting of the High Seventeen to Consider the Report of Captain Van Kloop and Other Company Matters

Assembled this day, *Zeventien Herren* the Seventeen Most High Directors of the *Oost-Indische Compagnie* in the great Hall of Amsterdam, Lord Protect Us, March the 8th, 1726.

(Dressed in expensive woolen and silk suits, scented powdered wigs, some smoking carved clay pipes or Brazilian cigars, the enormously wealthy directors gathered around a large polished table to discuss the affairs of the Company. Behind each director was a clerk, who stood at attention to do their bidding. The walls of the ornate hall were hung with paintings of Rembrandt, Van Eyk and other masters of the "Golden Age.")

Secretary Meuse reads the agenda:

Item: The Company's return to investors averaged 29 percentum for the year 1725, down 3 percentum from the profits for the previous year.

Item: The following ships have been lost:

The *Zwelynk*, bound for Batavia, lost somewhere off the coast of the Land of Endrecht (Western Australian Reef), four months overdue in Batavia.

The *Zeeland,* outbound to Deshima, lost in a storm off the coast of Capetown with all hands.

The *Cormandel,* fully laden, taken by French pirates east of the Azores

The *Hague,* captured by Barbary muslims off the Moroccan Coast, the Captain killed, most of the crew sold into slavery.

Item: The Company presently employs over 30,000 servants including militia, sailors, merchants, etc. Since competition is increasing from French and English merchants it is decided not to increase the salaries of servants this year.

Item: The price of pepper having dropped due to an oversupply and to diminished markets, it is resolved to destroy one third of the pepper trees in the Molucca plantations and to burn 3000 tonnes of pepper stored in our Amsterdam warehouses.

Item: Because of increasing insubordination among seamen and the increase in foreign seamen aboard Company vessels, it is resolved to increase fines for minor offenses and to request officers to treat their men with greater severity.

Item: Foreign competition for the East Indian carrying trade is becoming keener. The English, French and Danish governments have increased subsidies to their national trading companies. It is resolved to ask the Dutch States-General for additional subsidies.

Item: The coffee situation presents grave difficulties; it is out of hand, and a new policy must be formulated. Director Nicholas Witsen's effort to introduce coffee growing into Java has met with too great a horticultural success. The first few plants were sent by him to Batavia in 1707 and distributed to our allies in Matram and Bantam. In 1711, Java shipped 100 pounds of coffee to Holland. This brought a very high price. By 1720, the crop came to 100,000 pounds. Many local rulers have introduced it on their plantations and have become unseemingly wealthy to the detriment of the Company. In 1723, 12 million pounds of coffee beans were shipped from Java, and there is no end in sight.

Our policy has always been to deal in high-priced commodities whose supply we could monopolize and control. If we let the production of coffee further expand, we will have to seek broader markets, build more ships and warehouses and engage in a type of trade fit only for low-priced products and large markets. Therefore it is decreed that the production of coffee in the East Indies be restricted. A high tax will be placed on the producers of coffee. In addition, one out of every four plantations should be plowed under.

Item: The case of bookkeeper Jan Svilt, accused of unnatural acts, has been brought to our attention by Predikant Flugal. The man Svilt was put ashore on Ascension Island by order of the Commander and Captains of our homebound fleet. This punishment was decided on after a fair trial in accordance with Company prescribed procedures. His widow has petitioned the Company for information and relief. Appended is the Ship's Log containing the proceedings of the trial and Svilt's confession. Appended is Captain van Kloop's report and answer to Predikant Flugal's accusations of leniency. We find that the Captain acted in the best interest of the Company. Svilt's blood is not on our head. Amen.

Report of Captain van Kloop to the Heeren XVII.

On board from Batavia with us was the Predikant Flugal who complained that the sailors on our ship cursed, swore, whored and debauched more vilely than any other seamen he had encountered. He claimed that murder was a mere trifle to them. He entreated us to be more severe with the men and to beat them like donkeys, and that if we did not crack down on them with severe punishments, our own lives would be in danger. I, and most of the other officers on board, feel that the Predikant, who is known to you, exaggerates the case. Of course the sailors in our service are a rough lot. We pay them less than the navy; an able-bodied sailor receives only eleven guilders a month, which is hardly enough to live on. We do not draw the best men.

Flugal complained to you that "the men of the *Geertruyd* act like untamed boars; they rob and steal, drink and go whoring shamelessly, and are wantonly capable of beating up anybody." We feel that our men were no better and no worse than the common run of sailors. We maintain good discipline. We threaten when we have to, and beat recalcitrant men with the rope ends **when they do not instantly follow our officers' orders.**

Our sailors live a hard life. Seven of our men lost their lives falling from the yards during our last voyage. Many more died of scurvy. They must load and unload the ships like donkeys; while on board they are treated like slaves by our officers. Our men are well trained; they wait with hat in hand on the gangway whenever their officers walk off or on the ships.

We punish our men as severely as do most other officers.

Three men were keel-hauled in the Straits of Molucca for refus-ing to obey an order; a sailor who was caught stealing had his hand nailed to the mainmast; ten men were flogged off Madagascar for shitting below decks instead of in the head during a storm; seven men were put in irons on bread and water for complaining about the rations; 12 men were flogged for various other infractions. We have collected fines amounting to 220 guilders for blasphemy, drunkenness, insubordination, and other infractions of the Company's rules.

Regarding the case of Jan Svilt, we have submitted a copy of the log which includes the trial. We felt that it would be too harsh a punishment to tie Svilt and Bandino together and throw them overboard to the sharks as was suggested by Predikant Flugal. We feel that our punishment of Svilt was sufficient under the eyes of God.

We recommend that Bandino not be allowed to land in Holland, an act which would automatically make him a free Dutch citizen, but that he be shipped back to Batavia.

Respectfully, your servant,
Jo. van Kloop, Captain of the *Geertruyd*

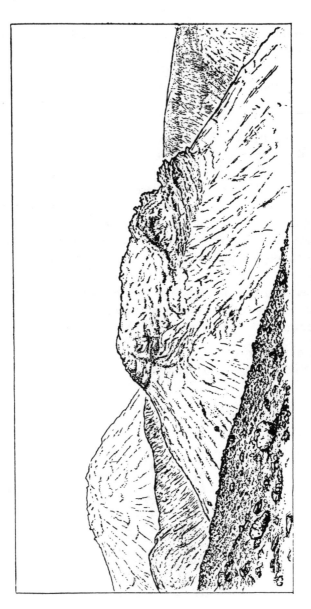

Ascension Island—a bleak prospect

XXIV. The End of the Voyage

September the 1st I killed another turtle; but having broke my hatchet I crushed the poor creature to pieces and raking among the entrails broke the gall, which made the blood very bitter; but was forced to drink it or should have died. My thoughts were bent upon another world, and the ardent desire to meet approaching death both cherished and tortured my departing soul. I soon vomited up again what I had before drunk.

I was parched throughout my body and drank a quart of salt water but could not contain it. I was so ill after it, that I expected immediate death, and prepared myself as best I could; I hope Jesus will have mercy on my soul. After it was dark I saw a turtle crawling toward my tent in the moonlight. I killed her and drank about two quarts of her blood. I then endeavored to sleep.

On the 3rd I awoke and, finding myself something better, employed my time in fitting a helve to my hatchet and eat some of the turtle which I had killed the night before.

From the 4th to the 6th I lived upon turtle blood and eggs.

l lay down in despair and fell into a fitful sleep. After a while l dreamed that as l walked through the wilderness full of hardships l came upon a place where there was a cave, and l laid me down in that place to rest. l dreamed that l was sadder than at any time in my life; all my sin and vileness appeared before me great and consuming. l saw that l was fit for nothing but hell and for the everlasting damnation of my soul — and l despaired. Then, suddenly l saw before me the Lord Jesus who looked down from **heaven and said to me in a gentle voice,** "Believe in the Lord Jesus Christ and thou shalt be saved." But l could only whisper "l am a great, a monstrous sinner." He smiled and answered, "My grace is sufficient for thee." At this my heart was full of joy. He said to me, "**You will reach the** Celestial City. Look, it is over yonder," and he pointed above. "Follow me." And l did, and as l entered the golden gates l was given a raiment of golden cloth, light as spiders' down. We were met by sweet angels with harps and flutes who sang the praise of God . . . **The city spires shone** like gold, the streets were paved with sunlight. ln the radiant streets walked men and women wearing crowns on their heads, carrying palm fronds in their hands. All were singing hymns of praise . . . Then l awoke to find two rats nibbling at my sandals.

7th September. I cannot live long; and I hope the Lord will have mercy on my soul. My strength decays.

The 8th, drank my own urine and ate raw flesh.

The 9th, 10th and 11th, I am so much decayed that I am a perfect skeleton; and cannot write the particulars, my hand shakes so. I resign my soul wholly to Providence.

The 12th, 13th, 14th, 15th, 16th and 17th, lived as before.

The 18th, 19th, 20th, 21st, 22nd, 23rd, 24th, 25th, 26th, 27th, 28th, 29th, 30th, October the 1st, 2nd, 3rd, 4th, 5th and 6th, all as before. Nothing.

The 7th, my wood is all gone, so that I am forced to **eat raw flesh and salted fowls. I cannot live long; and I** hope the Lord will have mercy on my soul. The 8th, drank my own urine and ate raw flesh.

The 9th, 10th, 11th, 12th, 13th and 14th, all as before....

THE JUST VENGEANCE OF HEAVEN EXEMPLIFIED, IN A JOURNAL LATELY FOUND BY CAPTAIN MAWSON, (COMMANDER OF THE SHIP COMPTON) ON THE ISLAND OF ASCENSION; AS HE WAS HOMEWARD-BOUND FROM INDIA. IN WHICH IS A FULL AND EXACT RELATION OF THE AUTHOR'S BEING SET ON SHORE THERE (BY ORDER OF THE COMMODORE AND CAPTAINS OF THE DUTCH FLEET) FOR A MOST ENORMOUS CRIME HE HAD BEEN GUILTY OF, AND THE EXTREME AND UNPARALL'D HARDSHIPS, SUFFERINGS, AND MISERY HE ENDUR'D, FROM THE TIME OF BEING LEFT THERE, TO THAT OF HIS DEATH. ALL WROTE BY HIS OWN HAND, AND FOUND LYING NEAR HIS SKELETON.

New-York: Printed and sold by James Parker at the New Printing-Office in Beaver-Street.   1747.

ADDENDA

A. Biblical references to homosexuality

B. Legal status and attitudes of various societies towards inversion

C. Ascension Island — History and present status

D. Thirst and dessication

E. Observations of Charles Darwin (1836) and other explorers of Ascension

BIBLICAL REFERENCES TO INVERSION

OLD TESTAMENT

Gen. 18;24
Gen. 18;24
The destruction of Sodom and Gemorrah.

Deut. 22;5
Anti-transvestite injunction; "Neither shall the man put on a woman's garb, it is an abomination . . ."

Lev. 18;22
The death penalty is prescribed for homosexuals and transvestites.

Lev. 19:22
"Thou shalt not lie with mankind as with womankind: it is an abomination."

Lev. 19;25
". . . the land is defiled, therefore I do visit the impurity thereof uponit and the land itself vomiteth out her inhabitants."

Lev. 20;13
"If a man lie with mankind as he lieth with a woman, both of them have committed an abomination: they shall surely be put to death; their blood shall be upon them."

Judges 19;22-25
The Lord destroyed Gibea and decimated Dan because the Gibeans desired to "know" men guests. They settled for a girl whom they then abused. The other eleven tribes of Israel virtually destroyed Dan for the offense.

I Kings 14;24, I Kings 15;12, I Kings 22;46
Mentions Sodomites, who engaged in abominations. Israelite rulers periodically exterminated Sodomites.

II Kings 23;7
Josiah destroyed Sodomites.

NEW TESTAMENT

I Corinthians 6.9
St. Paul's Epistle: "Know ye not that the unrighteous shall not inherit the Kingdom of God. Be not deceived: neither fornicators nor idolators, nor adulterers, nor effeminate, nor abusers of themselves with mankind.

6.13 "Meats for the belly, and the belly for meats, but God shall destroy both it and them. Now the body is not for fornication, but for the Lord; and the Lord for the body."

6.19 "What? know ye not that your body is the temple of the Holy Ghost which is in you, which ye have of God, and ye are not your own."

I, Timothy
"The law is not made for the righteous man, but for the lawless and disobedient, for the godless and for the sinners."

I. Timothy 1.10
"For the whoremongers, for them that defile themselves with mankind, for manstealers, for liars, for perjured persons and if there be any other thing contrary to sound doctrine."

6.7 "For we brought nothing into this world, and it is certain we can carry nothing out."

6.9 "But they that be rich fall into temptation and a snare and into many foolish and hurtful lusts which drown men in destruction and perdition."

I, Timothy 6.10
"For the love of money is the root of all evil: which while some coveteth after, they have erred from the faith, and pierced themselves through with many sorrows."

Romans (Paul's Epistle)

18 "For the wrath of God is revealed from heaven against all ungodliness . . ."

27 And likewise also the men, leaving the natural use of women, burned in their lust one toward another; men with men working that which is unseemly, and receiving in themselves that recompense of their error which was meet."

Legal Status and Attitudes
of Various Societies Towards Inversion

In the spring of 1976 the U.S. Supreme Court upheld a Virginia law against consensual sodomy ruling to adopt the decision of a lower three-judge Federal panel that decided that a state prohibition of sexual conduct "against nature" does not violate constitutional guarantees of due process, privacy, freedom of expression and freedom from cruel and unusual punishment. This decision will frustrate attempts to overthrow similar laws in other states on these grounds.

The lower court cited Biblical prohibitions, among others, against homosexuality to emphasize the long standing of such prohibitions and to show that society has the right to make such prohibitions.

Homosexuality in Other Societies and Times

Plato and his friends displayed an attitude towards love between men that often took a sexual form. Solon, Aristides, Sappho Xenephon, Pindar and other great classical Greeks attest to the popular acceptance of homosexuality—both between women and between men—in Greece.

The Spartans went further than the Athenians; they institutionalized phasic homosexuality in their army. Every young Spartan male was taken into the Army and expected to shun marriage and the company of women until he was discharged many years later. In Thebes, the best warriors were the "Sacred Band"—a famous regiment made up of 150 pairs of male lovers. This great fighting force defeated the Spartans at the Battle of Tegyrae in 375 B.C., and then again at Leuctra in 371. At the Battle of Chaeronea in 338 B.C., Philip of Macedonia annihilated the band, which paved the way for the fall of Democratic Greece to the barbarians.

Lucretius, Catullus, Virgil, Juvenal and other Roman poets took homosexuality for granted, although not at the same esthetic level as it had been in Greece. Plutarch's descriptions of love between males are stated as matter of course.

The early Christians myopic concern with an afterlife caused them to downgrade all physical pleasures. Christian emperors took political control of Rome in the 4th century, more than a hundred years before Rome fell to Odoacer in 476. Anti-homosexuality laws were introduced five years after the death of Constantine. Some fifty years later, the Christian emperor Theodocious I issued an edict condemning homosexuals to be burnt at the stake.

In the East, Byzantium lasted a thousand years longer than Rome, and in general took a more relaxed view towards homosexuality. However during a period of upheaval and panic following a series of plagues and earthquakes, the Emperor Justinian issued a Novella (A.D. 538) in which he implied that homosexuals were to blame for the catastrophes—i.e., that God was punishing the Empire as He had Sodom. We hear little of overt homosexuality in Byzantium until Constantinople fell to the Turks in 1453. Under Islamic rule, the homosexual minorities of the Balkans enjoyed relative toleration for 400 years.

Sexual deviates in Christian Europe were hanged, burned, drowned and starved with pious inhumanity. In Plymouth colony, approximately one quarter of all prosecutions for sexual offenses involved homosexuality. The Dutch Colony of New York included burning at the stake as a punishment for deviates. For the greater glory of God.

Though castigated in the Bible and prohibited in Jewish and Christian tradition, homosexuality has been permitted (and in some societies has been condoned) by many ancient and non-western cultures. But in the United States all fifty states follow English law and prohibit ''unnatural'' sexual conduct. Nevertheless these laws have been struck down in 15 states.

In Western Europe and Latin America the courts have abolished laws governing sexual conduct between consenting adults in private. Such reforms generally followed the Napoleonic code promulgated after the French Revolution.

The present legal position of American homosexuals is confused and applied by different states helter skelter. Sodomy laws are enforced extensively against two men, but not against a man and a woman. Prosecution for homosexual solicitation is much more frequent than prosecution for the actual perfomance of the acts themselves. Many companies and agencies still regard homosexuality as a moral bar against hiring and advancement.

Ascension Island

When first discovered by Portuguese sailors in the 16th century, Ascension, newly risen from the Mid-Atlantic ridge, was a gray volcanic heap covered with razor-sharp lava and volcanic cones. Sailors stopped there only out of dire necessity to repair their ships (see the account of Dampier) or to catch turtles. Desolation lay on the waterless island; it was shunned by man and beast.

Sea birds and turtles colonized at first. It remained completely uninhabited until 1815, when the British garrisoned it with marines in order to guard Napoleon exiled on St. Helena, 800 miles to the south.

In 1821, the year Napoleon died, the island assumed another role—it became the base for ships engaged in suppressing the slave trade originating in West Africa. Freed slaves and the men who hunted down the slavers used it as a sanatorium. The British Navy patrolled the entire African Coast from Cape Verde to Benguela in the south. Most of the illicit trade came out of the sector of the Bights of Benin and Biafra, some eight to ten days' sail from Ascension.

In the 1860's Lloyd's of London paid six pounds a year to a local Marine lookout who was stationed permanently on Cross Hill and whose job it was to report movement of steam ships. The reports reached London a month or more after the event.

But in 1899 Ascension acquired its first submarine cable from the Cape and St. Helena and so became a crossroad of international communications. Ever since, a cable station has been manned by the Eastern Telegraph Company. In 1922, administration of the island was turned over to the British Cable Company.

During World War II the United States constructed a landing strip for airplanes (see page 96), and the island population rose from 200 to 300.

In the 1960's the U.S. National Aeronautical & Space Agency (NASA) established a satellite tracking station 1750 feet above sea level, on the Devil's ashpit.

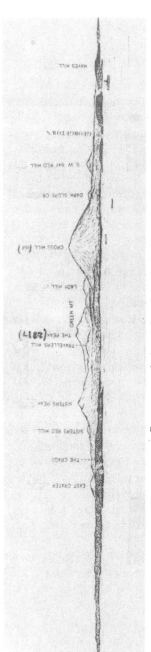

Panorama of Ascension Island, looking southeast from anchorage at Georgetown; from photograph.

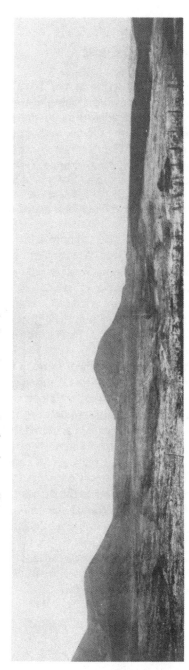

Looking west from Green Mountain road; left, lower slope of Lady Hill; middle, Cross Hill; right, young basaltic flow which issued from base of Sisters Peak.

Thirst and Desiccation

Thirst is a sensation common to all animals which have lost body fluids. Thirst forces the animal to seek relief in drinking. In its more extreme forms thirst is accompanied by a distressful feeling of dryness and heat localized in the throat and stomach along with parched lips and tongue. In the final stages of the agony the thirsty man's skin shrivels and the blood thickens, a condition which inhibits bleeding. Cases have been reported where desicated wanderers in the dessert with deep wounds did not bleed until they reached civilization and were given water.

Loss of body fluids which leads to thirst is increased when the surrounding air is above 98° Fahrenheit. A dry wind increases the fluid loss. Body fluids must be replenished in order for the blood to circulate and life to continue.

A healthy person requires about three liters of water per day to keep his metabolism working properly. The average American living in a technological society uses about 200 litres per day to flush his toilet, wash his clothes, bathe, rinse his car, etc. 220,000 liters of water are required to produce a ton of steel, 120,000 to distill one ton of petroleum, . . .

OBSERVATIONS OF CHARLES DARWIN WHO LANDED ON ASCENSION IN 1836 DURING HIS CIRCUMNAVIGATION OF THE GLOBE ABOARD THE BEAGLE, AND OTHER EXPLORERS

In 1836 Charles Darwin,* then a 27-year old fledgling naturalist, stopped at Ascension. He was on the last leg of his momentous voyage of discovery around the world aboard the Beagle, a three-masted bark with a burden of 242 tons. The description of Ascension which follows is taken from his *Voyage of the Beagle* and gives us a view of the island which had changed little since the time of Svilt.

On the 19th of July we reached Ascension. Those who have beheld a volcanic island, situated under an arid climate, will at once be able to picture to themselves the appearance of Ascension. They will imagine smooth conical hills of a bright red colour, with their summits generally truncated, rising separately out of a level surface of black rugged lava. A principal mound in the centre of the island, seems the father of the lesser cones. It is called Green Hill; its name being taken from the faintest tinge of that colour, which at this time of the year is barely perceptible from the anchorage. To complete the desolate scene, the black rocks on the coast are lashed by a wild and turbulent sea.

During the days when the English Navy ruled the waves Ascension was commissioned as a ship of the line and manned with British marines. Hence there was a small "establishment" referred to by Darwin.

The settlement is near the beach; it consists of several houses and barracks placed irregularly, but well built of white freestone. The only inhabitants are marines, and some negroes liberated from slave-ships, who are paid and victualled by government. There is not a private person on the island. Many of the marines appeared well contented with their situation; they

---

* Darwin was prone to seasickness which made his four years at sea most miserable.

132

think it better to serve their one-and-twenty years on shore, let it be what it may, than in a ship; in this choice, if I were a marine, I should most heartily agree.

The next morning I ascended Green Hill, 2840 feet high, and thence walked across the island to the windward point. A good cart-road leads from the coast-settlement to the houses, gardens, and fields, placed near the summit of the central mountain. On the roadside there are milestones, and likewise cisterns, where each thirsty passer-by can drink some good water. Similar care is displayed in each part of the establishment, and especially in the management of the springs, so that a single drop of water may not be lost: indeed the whole island may be compared to a huge ship kept in first-rate order. I could not help, when admiring the active industry which had created such effects out of such means, at the same time regretting that it had been wasted on so poor and trifling an end. M. Lesson has remarked with justice, that the English nation alone would have thought of making the island of Ascension a productive spot; any other people would have held it as a mere fortress in the ocean.

Near this coast nothing grows; further inland, an occasional green castor-oil plant, and a few grasshoppers, true friends of the desert, may be met with. Some grass is scattered over the surface of the central elevated region, and the whole much resembles the worse parts of the Welsh mountains. But scanty as the pasture appears, about six hundred sheep, many goats, a few cows and horses, all thrive well on it. Of native animals, land-crabs and rats swarm in numbers. Whether the rat is really indigenous, may well be doubted; there are two varieties as described by Mr. Waterhouse; one is of a black colour, with fine glossy fur, and lives on the grassy summit; the other is brown-coloured and less glossy, with longer hairs, and lives near the settlement on the coast. Both these varieties are one-third smaller than the common black rat (M. rattus); and they differ from it both in the colour and character of their fur, but in no other essential respect. I can hardly doubt that these rats (like the common mouse, which has also run wild) have been imported, and, as at the Galapagos, have varied from the

133

effect of the new conditions to which they have been exposed: hence the variety on the summit of the island differs from that on the coast. Of native birds there are none; but the guinea-fowl, imported from the Cape de Verd Islands, is abundant, and the common fowl has likewise run wild. Some cats, which were originally turned out to destroy the rats and mice, have increased, so as to become a great plague. The island is entirely without trees, in which, and in every other respect, it is very far inferior to St. Helena.

Darwin examined the strange geology and rocks of Ascension:

One of my excursions took me towards the S.W. extremity of the island. The day was clear and hot, and I saw the island, not smiling with beauty, but staring with naked hideousness. The lava streams are covered with hummocks, and are rugged to a degree which, geologically speaking, is not of easy explanation. The intervening spaces are concealed with layers of pumice, ashes, and volcanic tuff. Whilst passing this end of the island at sea, I could not imagine what the white patches were with which the whole plain was mottled; I now found that they were sea-fowl, sleeping in such full confidence, that even in mid-day a man could walk up and seize hold of them. These birds were the only living creatures I saw during the whole day. On the beach a great surf, although the breeze was light, came tumbling over the broken lava rocks.

The geology of this island is in many respects interesting. In several places I noticed volcanic bombs, that is, masses of lava which have been shot through the air whilst fluid, and have consequently assumed a spherical or pear-shape. Not only their external form, but, in several cases, their internal structure shows in a very curious manner that they have revolved in their aërial course. The internal structure of one of these bombs, when broken, is represented very accurately in the wood-cut on the next page. The central part is coarsely cellular, the cells decreasing in size towards the exterior; where there is a shell-like case about the third of an inch in thickness, of compact stone, which again is overlaid by the outside crust of finely cellular lava. I think there can be little doubt, first,

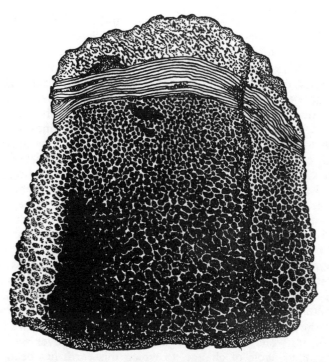

that the external crust cooled rapidly in the state in which we now see it; secondly, that the still fluid lava within, was packed by the centrifugal force, generated by the revolving of the bomb, against the external cooled crust, and so produced the solid shell of stone; and lastly, that the centrifugal force, by relieving the pressure in the more central parts of the bomb, allowed the heated vapours to expand their cells, thus forming the coarsely cellular mass of the centre.

A hill, formed of the older series of volcanic rocks, and which has been incorrectly considered as the crater of a volcano, is remarkable from its broad, slightly hollowed, and circular summit having been filled up with many successive layers of ashes and fine scoriæ. These saucer-shaped layers crop out on the margin, forming perfect rings of many different colours, giving to the summit a most fantastic appearance;

one of these rings is white and broad, and resembles a course round which horses have been exercised; hence the hill has been called the Devil's Riding School. I brought away specimens of one of the tufaceous layers of a pinkish colour; and it is a most extraordinary fact, that Professor Ehrenberg[7] finds it almost wholly composed of matter which has been organized: he detects in it some siliceous-shielded, fresh-water infusoria, and no less than twenty-five different kinds of the siliceous tissue of plants, chiefly of grasses. From the absence of all carbonaceous matter, Professor Ehrenberg believes that these organic bodies have passed through the volcanic fire, and have been erupted in the state in which we now see them. The appearance of the layers induced me to believe that they had been deposited under water, though from the extreme dryness of the climate I was forced to imagine, that torrents of rain had probably fallen during some great eruption, and that thus a temporary lake had been formed, into which the ashes fell. But it may now be suspected that the lake was not a temporary one. Anyhow, we may feel sure, that at some former epoch, the climate and productions of Ascension were very different from what they now are. Where on the face of the earth can we find a spot, on which close investigation will not discover signs of that endless cycle of change, to which this earth has been, is, and will be subjected?

[7] [Darwin] Monats. der König. Akad. d. Wiss. zu Berlin. Vom April, 1845.

In the 1920's the American geologist Reginald Daly headed an exploration of Ascension, the results of which were printed in the 1925 Proceedings of the American Academy of Arts and Science. Included herein is his topographical map of the island.

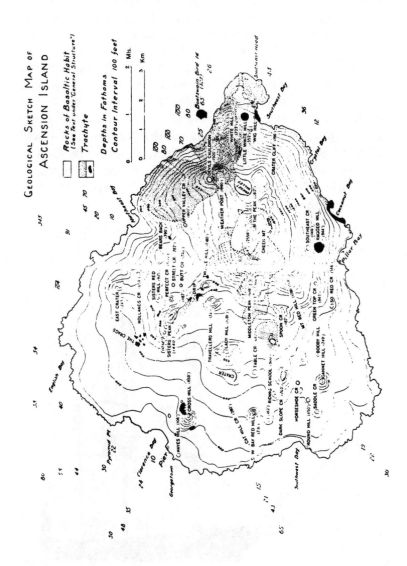

GEOLOGICAL SKETCH MAP OF ASCENSION ISLAND

Rocks of Basaltic Habit (See Text under 'General Structure')

Trachyte

Depths in Fathoms
Contour Interval 100 feet

Ascension Island sits atop the Mid Atlantic Ridge which runs along a line stretching down the Atlantic Ocean and marks the edge of separation zone between the techtonic plates of Eurasia-Africa and the Americas.

The ridge is 300 to 600 miles wide and some 10,000 miles long beginning north of Iceland and stretching around South Africa. Most of the ridge is 5000 to 10,000 feet above the Atlantic Basin but, in a few spots its peaks thrust up to form the Islands of the Azores, the Rocks of St. Paul, Ascension, St. Helena, Tristan da Cunha, Bouvert and most recently the new island of Surtstey. The highest peak on Pico Island in the Azores is 8000 feet above sea level.

H.M.S. Beagle

MAJOR REFERENCES

BLOK, P.J.: *History of the People of the Netherlands.* 5 volumes, N.Y., London, 1898, *et sub.*

BONNER, W.H.: *Capt. William Dampier.*

BOXER, C.R.: *The Dutch Seaborne Empire*, Knopf, 1965.

DALY, R.A.: *The Geology of Ascension Island.* 1975, Proc. Amer. Acad. Arts &Science.

DAMPIER, WILLIAM: *A New Voyage Around the World.*

EPSTIEN, L.M.: *Sex Laws and Customs, 1968.*

HAMILTON, ALEXANDER: *A New Account of the East Indies (1688-1723)*, Argonaut Press, 1930.

HART-DAVIS, DUFF: *Ascension*, 244 p., 1973, Double-Day.

HYMA, A.: *The Dutch In the Far East*, Ann ARbor, 1942, 249 p.

SCHAMTER, W. (1638-1704): *Voyage Aux Indes Orientals 1658*, 2 vols., published 1725.

VLEKKE, B.H.M.: *Nusantara—A History of E. Indies Archipelago*, 1943.

VLEKKE, B.H.M.: *Evolution of the Dutch Nation, N.Y., 1945.*

INDEX